My Heart Goes Home

Thomas Lossing and wife Elizabeth Gurnee Lossing at home in Berkeley, Calif., in the 1930s.

My Heart Goes Home

A HUDSON VALLEY MEMOIR

by
Thomas Sweet Lossing

edited by
Peter D. Hannaford

My Heart Goes Home: A Hudson Valley Memoir

First Edition, 1997

Published by
Purple Mountain Press, Ltd.
Main Street, P.O. Box E3
Fleischmanns, New York 12430-0378
Tel.: 914-254-4062
Fax: 914-254-4476
E-mail: Purple@catskill.net

Library of Congress Cataloging-in-Publication Data

Lossing, Thomas Sweet, b. 1872
    My heart goes home : a Hudson Valley memoir / by Thomas Sweet
Lossing : edited by Peter D. Hannaford. - - 1st ed.
        p.   cm.
    ISBN 0-935796-87-8 (pbk. : alk. paper)
    1. Lossing, Thomas Sweet, b. 1872- -childhood and youth.
2. Dutchess County (N.Y.)- -Social life and customs.   3. Dutchess
County (N.Y.)- -Biography.   4. Hudson River Valley (N.Y. and N.J.)-
-Social life and customs.   5. Hudson River Valley (N.Y. and N.J.)-
-Biography.   6. Lossing, Benson John, 1813-1891.   I. Hannaford,
Peter.   II. Title.
    F127.D8L69   1997
    974.7'33041'092   97-14258
    [B]- -DC21   CIP

Manufactured in the United States of America on acid-free paper.
5 4 3 2 1

FOREWORD

My Heart Goes Home is the account of a happy boy-hood in a vanished time—the 1870s and '80s—in Dutchess County, New York. Thomas Sweet Lossing was born at his family's farm, "The Ridge," on Chestnut Ridge above Dover Plains on October 3, 1872, the son of Benson J. and Helen Sweet Lossing.

This memoir, written in the 1930s after Thomas had retired in California, evokes the sights, sounds and smells of rural Hudson Valley life so sharply that one feels transported to that time and place on reading it.

Thomas's father, Benson, was a popular and widely read historian, a man of letters with a wide range of acquaintances in the worlds of public and literary af-

i

fairs. (General Lew Wallace of Civil War fame, visited the Lossings at The Ridge and is said to have written parts of *Ben Hur* there.) Benson was in his 60th year when Thomas was born. Thomas recalls both his parents with great warmth, and tells the story of a loving family, its relatives and neighbors. He also tells us of tradespeople and hard-scrabble farmers, struggling to survive.

Benson Lossing was over 40 years of age when he started his family with Helen, his second wife (his first wife, Alice Barritt, a writer, died in 1855, after 22 years of marriage. They had no surviving children). Benson and Helen's children were Edwin, Alice, Thomas and Miriam (who, as Helen Lossing Johnson, became a well-known writer and illustrator of children's books). They died in 1911, 1912 and 1945, respectively.

The Lossing children spent happy hours in their father's library, with its 5,000 volumes, artwork, artist's equipment and many valued relics with historical significance.

Young Thomas was acutely observant—almost photographically so—and his memoirs evoke images of the library, of hired workers, animals, roads, hamlets, houses, and children at work and play. The Blizzard of '88, summer trips to New York City and to Fire Island, and the Dutchess County Fair—all are described from the perspective of a boy in the late 19th Century.

Thomas Lossing tells of manor houses and hovels, taverns, schools, churches, of homemade remedies, country doctors, barn-raisings, cheese factories, pet woodchucks and skunk-trapping. He knew organ-grinders and peddlers, such as Honest John, who traded tinware for scrap metal and never offered a fair price, and The Palm Leaf Peddler, a simpleminded fellow who successfully sold his linens and laces without ever uttering a word.

Young Thomas saw many strange Hudson Valley

characters come and go, such as The Old Bone Picker, an ancient, dirty fellow from Oniontown, who traveled around to collect bones of every description, and Orebed Amy, who had lost his mind when he lost his property, and spent the rest of his life digging holes around the countryside, searching for precious metal.

The Lossing and Sweet families trace their ancestries to the earliest European settlers in the American colonies, and Thomas's anecdotes, description and memories are of a 19th Century household that was much like the American ideal of its day: agrarian, patriotic, religious, sentimental, soundly educated, noble-spirited and, at the same time, down-to-earth and full of fun.

Thomas lived the rough-and-tumble farm boy's life, though he was the son of a distinguished man of letters and of a highly-cultured mother. Young Thomas was taught at home, for the most part, and much of his learning came from coping with the practical demands of country life.

He lived at The Ridge until leaving to study civil engineering. In the early part of this century he went to South America to work for the Cerro de Pasco Mining Company at La Fundicion, Peru. During his years there he married Rebecca and took her with him to the Andes to live. In 1913, they became friends with a young naturalist from Chicago's Field Museum, Malcolm Anderson, and his wife, Elizabeth. The Andersons were beginning an extended honeymoon, during which Malcolm would gather rare bird specimens for the museum.

During World War I the Lossings returned to the United States where Thomas became the superintendent of construction of Langley Field in Virginia. Not longer after, Rebecca died. Meanwhile, Malcolm Anderson had died in 1918 in an accident. Thomas and Elizabeth Anderson met again and were married on December 26, 1926. They lived in Berkeley, California where he died on May 20, 1944, in his 73rd year. He had no children by either marriage, but he was remembered by his nieces, nephews and many great-nieces and nephews as a warm and kindly man—just as he had remembered his father.

It was in Berkeley that, with the encouragement of Elizabeth, he recalled his Hudson Valley youth and let his heart go home.

Peter D. Hannaford
Washington, DC

TABLE OF CONTENTS

FOREWORD BY PETER D. HANNAFORD

The Ridge, ca. 1880s, with Thomas, Miriam, Benson, Helen, and Alice Lossing.

PROLOGUE

It was evening at The Ridge. The year was 1880. The supper dishes had been cleared, but the family lingered at the dining room table, smiling encouragingly at my little sister, Miriam, and me.

All those whom we loved best were in the room: our understanding father, lamplight shining on his white hair and beard and ruddy cheeks; our adored mother, her arms folded, sitting so straight in her chair, yet always with an air of gaiety, heightened that evening by an azalea leaf caught in her dark hair; our handsome older brother, Edwin, on vacation from Warren's Military Institute; and our older sister, Alice, whose black braids and brown cashmere basque swept the table as she leaned forward to rest her dark eyes upon us. And Hawkeye, our shepherd dog, who had succeeded in barking his way indoors that evening.

Sarah and Arnold

When all was quiet, Miriam stood up. Her white, long-sleeved apron, fastened down the back with buttons and apron strings, nearly covered her blue flannel dress. A circle comb held her dark hair away from her high forehead, and a pigtail came down to her shoulders. She held a small book made of brown wrapping paper. This was our "novel." We had titled it *Sarah and Arnold*. In a clear voice, Miriam began to read from it.

For weeks beforehand, at our small desk snuggled against our father's in the Upper Library, Miriam and I had labored on *Sarah and Arnold*. In addition to pens and pencils for writing, we had paint brushes, needle, thread and brown wrapping paper for completing the "publication" of our work. We had a sense of great importance at this undertaking.

Our aim had been to write a love story, but, as it turned out, we disliked our hero and heroine. Marion had written bad things about them and, in the illustrations for the book, I had drawn them with long, turned-up noses and patches on their clothes.

In one passage we had Arnold drive up to Sarah's door in a square, black wagon, with a whip in his hand. We wrote, "Sarah stepped out lightly," a phase that drew laughter from the family. Early in our story, the pair had a lovers' quarrel but, by the end, "They married and lived happily ever afterward."

We children glowed in our family's approval, and it is to the memory of a simple family evening like this— and to an infinite number of other memories—that my heart goes home.

Benson Lossing sketch of the northwest corner
of his library.

Chapter I
MY FATHER AND FAMILY

"Home" had been home for five generations of our family on Chestnut Ridge, eight hundred feet above sea
level and twenty miles east of the Hudson River. Our
farm, in Dutchess County, New York, was called The
Ridge, our house having been built in 1801 by my great
grandfather, Nehemiah Sweet, and his three sons.

The
Ridge

One of my earliest impressions is of my father going
down the long hall on the second floor that led from
his and my mother's bedroom. I was so little that he
seemed just a pair of legs vanishing up three or four
steps through the iron door into his study. Beyond that
door was a large room, with bookcases on all sides
full of books. There were tall, arched windows, a blank

white ceiling, and the floor was covered with brown manila matting.

In the morning the sun would be pouring into the study from the east. The view in this direction looked under the limbs of our large pine trees, across the meadow and up the Sharon Valley to Sharon, Connecticut. In the afternoon, the sun would be coming in the windows from the west. The view from these windows was across our sheep pastures, over the hills to the Shawangunk Mountains across the Hudson River valley.

In the hall just outside my father's study was a tall, eight-day Terry clock with upper and lower doors. Father would often take the keys to the clock out of his pocket and open the lower door to show us the heavy weights and the long pendulum swinging back and forth. Every eighth day came the ceremony of his winding the clock, and we never failed to be there to watch him turn the crank and see the weights go up.

My father was very often in his study by four in the morning and worked there until the family breakfast at seven. The meal began by mother leading in a silent blessing. Then we ate oatmeal, steak or ham and eggs, fried potatoes, coffee and toast and talked over what we were going to do that day and what the weather was. On cool mornings there was a log fire in the fireplace.

After the meal we all went into the library where Mother read a chapter in the Bible. Then Father would go into his study to work all morning. Mother looked after her garden and plants and household, and we young ones performed our little duties, such as watering our plants. When school age arrived we were at our lessons at nine o'clock. Until school age, most of our time was spent in play, outdoors in all clear weather.

My mother would tell me to be sure to come in be-

A Terry clock

After breakfast

fore the dew fell. One evening I heard the sunset gun at West Point, and I rushed to the window, thinking the dew must have just fallen!

In the summer we often went out to the meadow and gathered tiger lilies, the grass up to our necks and waving in the wind. It seemed like being in the ocean with the waves of grass sweeping over us, the bob-o-links swaying on the lilies in the wind. Early in summer, when the grass was short, the meadows were gay with yellow buttercups. We picked armfuls of flowers then and filled vases of the hall, library mantlepiece and piazza.

We all met for one o'clock dinner, hungry in spite of our hearty breakfast. Monday was what we called "gray dinner day," as it was laundry day for the cook. There was cold turkey or roast from Sunday, and floating island or cottage pudding. Mother would taste a spoonful of the dessert and say it was as good as ice cream, but we young ones didn't think so.

Midday meals

Tuesday, ironing day, was again somewhat of a "gray dinner," but Wednesday would be grand again, perhaps roast beef, mutton or veal, mashed potatoes, squash or beets, dandelion greens heaped high on a platter and topped with slices of hard-cooked egg, cup puddings which were made in a deep pudding dish with a cup upside down in the center to keep the crust from getting soggy, or Brown Betty, or apple or mince pie.

Thursday, Friday and Saturday were much the same. There was always homemade bread, home-churned butter, jams, jellies and often delicious wild fresh berries in season or preserved in winter. The height of the wild strawberry season was at Fourth of July.

After the midday meal, my father would go up to his study again, and by three o'clock my mother had settled down to read. We played croquet or swung in the big swing on the limb of a large maple tree. I used to put my cats, Tiger and Ulysses, in the swing, to their great discomfort. After two or three swings their eyes would

At play

get bleary and heavy and they made the most mournful and dreary howls. When they finally landed on the ground they were decidedly seasick.

My father wrote until about four in the afternoon in spring and early summer. He then came down to sit in his willow chair under the maple trees on the lawn and read the *Poughkeepsie Times*, the *New York Times*, the *Dutchess Farmer* and the *Amenia Times*.

Children reading

We children had *Harper's Young People* and Jacob Abbott's *Stories for Young People*. One of my favorites was "Handy Level," the good little boy who always thanked his mother for everything she mended. He fixed up the house for his mother, built a little water wheel for his playmates, and was a good boy generally. Adolphus was just the opposite. He was idle. He set fire to a corncrib. He was very bad and made other boys bad. I used to think he must have had a delightfully free life.

Supper brought us all together again. We had white and brown bread, milk or cambric tea, lettuce salad, rhubarb or apple sauce, field strawberries with cream and sugar, and plain cake and gingersnaps. In winter there might be cornbread and molasses.

A stroll

After haying time, when we had finished our supper (between six or seven) we all walked out to the ends of the long shadows of the spruce and maple trees, the sun low to the horizon.

My mother carried her yellow plaid shawl, my little sister in a white apron with her black pigtail hanging down into one of my father's hands, and I holding on to his other hand. My older sister pranced along, snorting like a horse.

Often we would all let loose of each other and make a sudden dive into a haycock, or we raced around in rings until we fell down through sheer exhaustion from laughter. By the time the sun set we had begun to return to the house. The dew was rising from the ground, and the most lovely smell from freshly cut grass came to us.

In many places, the ground was raised in little streaks where meadow moles were working under the sod. There often were little mounds of fresh earth at the portals of these tunnels. Hawkeye, our dog, was with us and sometimes made a dive to catch a meadow mole.

Hawkeye and moles

When we reached the house by dusk, the fireflies had begun to glow, the tree toads to murmur. As we sat on the porch, hop toads came out and made their little guttural noise. They came from under the stone horse block and hopped down the gravel path.

It turned cool while we sat on the porch. The tree toads made their noise in the trees, and there sometimes came distant rumbling. By now, the night was jet black except for the glow of the fireflies and the occasional heat lightning and forked lightning traveling from one thunderhead to another.

Then we heard the first distinct peal of thunder, more lightning, and nearer and nearer thunder. The leaves on the maple tree began to stir in the fresh breeze and a door slammed somewhere in the house. It was time for us to take in Ritter, our canary, who was perched in his cage on the porch, and to see all the windows were closed before the shower.

In the winter, Mother tended to her plants in the green room, and it was common to see azalea leaves stuck in her hair where she had brushed against them. Occasionally, she burned tobacco stems in an old tin cup to kill the rose bugs on her roses. On stormy days when school was closed, we kids made ourselves cozy in the library with our drawing and painting. Ulysses, the yellow cat, and Hawkeye would be with us. My older sister, if not drawing or painting, sat up on a high step-ladder exploring some old book and frequently laugh-

In the library

7

ing. On one of those occasions she found a picture in an old parchment- covered Dutch Bible, showing a man pulling a beam "from his brother's eye." The beam was represented as a long stick of timber.

We were allowed to look at any book in the library after we had been taught how to treat them. We loved the old, bound *Harper's* magazines and *Harper's Weekly*; Dore's Bibles, with their steel engravings, *Peterkin Papers*. *St. Nicholas* and *Chatterboxes*.

One beautifully bound blue leather book contained a story of a lover who had ridden off with his sweetheart behind him on his horse, her arms around his neck. He was talking sweetly to her, planning their future, but when he turned to look at her she had turned to a skeleton. I was always afraid to look at this picture, yet it fascinated me.

Still, I wasn't afraid of the small mummy crocodile and the skull of a colored man that, with other relics, were in a box in one of the cupboards.

Every weekday morning at about eleven o'clock the mailman rang the doorbell and we rushed for my father's mailbag.

Whoever got it first hurried upstairs to my father's study, the rest following, all out of breath as Father unstrapped the bag and pulled out the letters and magazines. We noticed the *Harper's Weekly* always looked as if it had been taken from its wrapper and put back in again. One day I found a woman's long, reddish brown hair on the inside pages of the magazine. Oddly enough, the postmistress had hair of the same color.

The mail

Other magazines were *Harper's Bazaar, Scribners, Farm Journal*, but it was *St. Nicholas* my older sister was looking for, and *Scientific American* my brother wanted, and *Harper's Young People* that my little sister and I were eager about. When we found it, we ran downstairs and she would read it to me.

At that time the main story running in *Harper's Young People* was "Toby Tyler," about a boy with his pet monkey traveling with a circus. One of the little songs in it that we loved was:

> Oh, I am so sleepy,
> I lie down to rest
> Here in the sun.
> Soon will he go
> To his bed in the West,
> Day will be done.
> Oh, I am so sleepy.

Songs for young ones

Whenever we felt sleepy we would sing this and lie down to rest. There was another song, with illustrations I liked so much when I was four or five years:

> I am the lad in the blue and white,
> Sing, hey, the merry sailor lad.
> My hand is steady, my step is light,
> My brave little heart, all right, all right,
> I am ready to dance, I am ready to fight,
> Sing, hey, the merry sailor lad.

A companion one began: "I am the lad in the blue and gray..." referring to the soldier boys of the Civil War.

Along about four o'clock on winter days my younger sister and I would crawl up the steps to my father's study on our hands and knees, so as not to make any noise. We gradually opened the door, crawled across the floor and under his desk and begin to tickle him on his knees. Father would twitch his legs and finally look under and would act so surprised. Then all three of us would laugh.

Father's study and desk

If my father was very busy he would look at us sternly

and we would keep quiet, but if he were not so busy he would let us look into his stamp box or he let us tear off the stamps from the perforated sheet and fill the box, which originally was a marble snuff box of some historic value.

There was a little drawer at the right hand of his desk containing pencils and dividers, a protractor, an old-type silver pencil and a box of its leads—so hard they would scarcely make a mark. The leads would jam way up in the pencil, and we would have to jar them to make them come out again. But it was fun to borrow the silver pencil and try to use it. This little drawer was always smutted from the pencils and leads rolling around in there.

There was a little sandpaper pack with a handle to use in sharpening the points of the pencils. When I would turn it away from me and shut it suddenly into its sheath it would shoot out a cloud of black dust, like a gun. In this drawer father also kept a hone for sharpening his penknife. We would often ask to borrow this knife and it was never refused us.

He would reach down in his pocket and, after he said we could have it, the thing was to get it, for he would hold it in the middle of his hand and when we reached for it he would stick out a finger, then a thumb, then another finger and we would giggle and laugh, squealing, "Now, Papa!"

In a corner just inside the door of the study were a gold-headed cane and a silver-headed cane. One had been made of timber from the frigate Constitution, the other of timber from the frigate Constellation. Another cane was of whalebone carved to represent a rope with a Turk's-head knot on top. This one had been made by a sailor on the Kane expedition in search of the North Pole. Still another cane was made of a brass tube, veneered on the outside with rosewood, a removeable cap on top. Inside was a very large, slimsy, green silk

*Canes
and
umbrellas*

10

umbrella, with an ivory handle. We young ones used to delight in drawing out the umbrella, opening it and sitting under it. Over the canes hung some wampum and an Indian bow with arrows.

In the study a large "revolving desk" (really only the top bookcase part revolved) stood near my father's desk. The desk part was given over to our use, and in it we kept white and yellow scrap paper in abundance, pens and pencils, crayons, watercolor paints and brushes. By pulling out one of the little drawers we could reach down and get the lemon that we felt was necessary to refresh us while at our literary labors. I also had a small green boat in there.

At this revolving desk and by the light of father's lamp, my sister and I wrote the novel we named, *Sarah and Arnold.* We composed it together, but the actual writing was done by my sister while my watercolors illustrated it. We wrote it on brown wrapping paper, folded in book form, six inches square, and the cover was decorated. The title was taken from a newspaper story running at the time.

Winter evenings found our family in the library, and if the wind was blowing a gale the Baltimore heater glowed. This kind of heater was very fashionable, especially in city houses. It was recessed into the fireplace, closed tight in front with doors, and fitted with isinglass so you could look in on the fire. It heated our library and my father's study upstairs.

On a winter night

On the center table we had a student lamp. We often all were seated around this table, and my mother or my older sister read aloud. Later, my younger sister read a great deal to my father. Reading was from Shakespeare, Dickens, *The Arabian Nights, Pilgrim's Progress*, Scott, Tennyson, and many others. I still remember shivering to hear Poe's poem "The Raven."

My father used his eyes so much during the day that

he often sat with them closed, even when we played checkers. He would keep his eyes shut and we had to tell him when it was his turn. We always beat him.

Parchesi was another favorite game, along with card games like Whist and Old Maid. When our little cousin was with us she used to slip the Old Maid into my father's hand as he was reaching out for a card with his eyes half shut. Then she squealed, "O, Uncle's the Old Maid!" My cousin had lots of fun with my father.

Favorite games

He wore his white hair long and combed down over his ears, the custom of men his age. My cousin would stand on a footstool and comb his hair, raise it up to look at his ears and, with a grin, show them to us.

Father sat with eyes shut all the time.

*The Ridge as it looked in the mid-1990s,
with the stone library at left.*

Chapter II
THE RIDGE

My grandfather, Nehemiah Sweet, and my great-uncles, Silas, John and Stephen, all had been engaged in the lumber business. When Grandfather selected Chestnut Ridge as the site for his house (near my great-grandmother's old home), Great Uncle Silas, on his trips by sloop to the lumber district of Port Edward, began selecting knot-free pine to be used for the siding and trim. The pine was rafted down to Poughkeepsie and hauled the twenty miles to Chestnut Ridge.

Grandfather Sweet's house

Grandfather's house was Colonial in design, the hewn oak frame erected over a cellar that had three-foot-thick foundation walls, with stone piers and logs beneath the kitchen hearth and brick oven. The floors were of pine, brought from Georgia. The laths were made of local chestnut, sawed first into half-inch boards, then split the other way. Handwrought nails were used on the siding, shingles and flooring. Handwrought brads were used in the trim.

The house was painted white. It had large windows with small panes. Green shutters, held by iron S's, framed the windows. The front of the porch was flanked by Doric columns and there were fluted pilasters on each side of the front doors and windows.

The first floor had a wide hall, staircase, parlor and a dining room with two bedrooms off it. A large passageway connected the dining room with the kitchen. Off the kitchen were a bedroom and a pantry, of equal size. The second floor also had a wide hall. Two large and two smaller bedrooms were off this hall. A staircase led to an immense attic up under the heavy oak rafters.

The parlor, dining room and the two large bedrooms upstairs were heated by fireplaces. Three quarters of the west wall of the kitchen was covered by a huge fireplace to which the brick oven was attached.

The new stone library

When my family lived in this house of Grandfather Sweet's, my parents made certain changes, adding a two-story stone library for my father, extending the downstairs hall, and adding a laundry that had two rooms above it. The attic was divided into four bedrooms. These alterations gave the house twenty-two rooms in all.

For extra heat, we added four stoves, installed the Baltimore heater in the Lower Library and put cookstoves in the kitchen and laundry. All of this required more than sixty feet of stovepipe!

For us young ones, the kitchen was a favorite place in the house to be.

Almira

Almira, our colored housekeeper, always had paper on the kitchen dresser shelves with the edges cut out in fancy shapes. The lowest shelf had a wooden Oswego starch box to hold the cooking forks and knives, and a place for tablecloths. Also on that shelf was a ginger snap box for the delicious ginger snaps that Almira frequently made. No limit was ever placed on the number we might have whenever we wished. We used to stampede the kitchen whenever we smelled them baking.

Ginger snaps and the kitchen

The next shelf above had a set of yellow earthenware mixing bowls and custard bowls to match; the blue china for the kitchen table, and a white bowl full of brown sugar. The shelf above that had small pitchers, some thick tumblers and a few odd dishes that were seldom used.

The kitchen was about twenty feet square. There was a window over the sink near the pump on the west, and the remainder of this side was taken up with an immense old fireplace and a brick oven. In this fireplace was a range that had been made to fit, and many a Thanksgiving dinner was cooked on it.

The south side of the kitchen had two windows and an outside door. A large square table under one of the windows was used for a work table. Its drawer contained a large and small ironing board and some flat-irons as well as a few spare iron muffin rings used as standards for the hot irons. Hanging over the table near the window was a box with rottenstone, used for scouring knives. On a corner of the table near the door was a large wooden pail made of cedar, with brass hoops (which were always scoured bright by Almira). The pail contained drinking water from the deep, cold well in the yard.

Potatoes were cooked in a three-legged iron pot, and the vigorous pounding when they were being mashed could be heard for a long distance. When the pounding was heard, it was the signal for us young ones to run and lick the wooden pounder when the job was

15

finished. Strange to say there was always a good deal of potato left on the pounder for us to lick. We would pass the pounder around and each one pushed off a fingerful then handed it to the next—actually, no "licking" was done.

The east side of the kitchen had a door leading into the pantry between the kitchen and dining room, off of which, on the right side, were cupboards where the white china for the dining room table was kept, and also the everyday silverware. To the left of this entry was a large woodbox for the dining room firewood, red oak. Here, too, was the entrance to the back stairs.

The next door from the kitchen on this side led downstairs to the cellar. On the north side was the door leading into the bedroom of Almira, her husband Jacob, and their daughter, Gertrude. Between this door and a door into a pantry was a cupboard full of chinaware of all description, as well as frying pans and a large pot with a tight cover for boiling ham. There was also a plum pudding tin with a hollow center. One cupboard, near the bedroom door and under the counter shelf, was reserved for Gertrude's paper dolls.

Shelves, pots and jugs

The pantry off the kitchen was large, with shelves on all sides, some of them with doors. Screwed fast to one of the sides of the cupboard was the coffee grinder. The sound of the grinder served as a rising bell for us young ones, as we could hear it even up on the third floor, where we slept.

On the shelves of the pantry were pans of milk with thick cream on top. There, too, was a large stone pot full of brown sugar, which we visited occasionally. On the floor under the shelves were immense stone pots, one containing sugar cookies, some solid and some with holes in the middle. This cookie pot was not supposed to be visited.

There were other smaller pots full of butter and lard. In a brown jug with a wooden cork wound with cloth, was homemade potato and hop yeast, which Almira used in making her delicious bread. The yeast was considered ready when the cork popped.

On the shelf under the window was a set of scales that could weigh up to a hundred pounds and was used for portioning cakes and plum puddings and Christmas cookies. Mother always superintended the making of the Christmas cookies, which were rather hard, but delicious, with a sprinkling of caraway seeds through them. They were from my great grandmother's recipe. Rolled and cut out, some of them were stamped with the old wooden eagle pattern that had belonged to her.

Cookies and molds

We also had some of my great grandmother's tin cookie molds. One was a large bird with square feet, and a dried currant had to be used for its eye. Two other patterns were smaller, one being heart-shaped and the other a diamond with a scalloped edge. Mother also cut out crullers in square shapes, using a jiggering iron, decorations being cut in the center with the same iron.

In one corner of the large (ten by fifteen foot) pantry was a small table used for a molding board. There was a little drawer in it for the rolling pin and muffin rings. In another corner were two flour barrels, one for white, one for graham flour. The floor of this pantry had wide Georgia pine boards, six inches across, which Almira always kept scoured clean. The kitchen floor was also of Georgia pine boards, kept just as immaculately clean.

In the kitchen was the servants' dining table, on the center of which was a kerosene lamp. The woodwork of the kitchen was grained to represent oak; the ceiling was plaster, whitewashed, and the walls were painted light gray. On the west side, over the brick oven and the fireplace, was a long wooden mantle with five cupboards over it. In the cupboard toward the south side were small household tools and tools for mend-

17

ing harnesses, and tallow mixed with lampblack for greasing leather boots. This sort of work was often done on stormy days.

Between this cupboard and the next one stood a flat, high clock with an open face, striking the hour on a gong. The next cupboard had flatirons and the like. Still another had shoe blacking, stove polish and brushes. The fourth cupboard never had much of anything in it, being farther from the light. The last and fifth one never had anything in it because the hinges were broken, fastened up and painted over.

As a little boy I used to think these cupboards led to mysterious places, or maybe even to Heaven.

In front of the kitchen fireplace was a broad brick hearth, and at each end of the hearth was a square slate stone. This immense hearth and chimney were supported on strong stone buttresses in the cellar, capped with heavy hewn timbers that formed bins for apples, potatoes and other vegetables.

Views from the Ridge

The Ridge originally had comprised nine hundred acres, but in our time we had the best of these in more than three hundred and forty acres. To the west of Chestnut Ridge, beyond our sheep pastures and hills, we had a sweeping view of the mountains across the Hudson. To the northeast, we looked up the Sharon Valley to Sharon, Connecticut.

Beyond the large open meadow to the east, we could see higher, rolling fields sloping toward the north, and through the blue haze in the distance we could make out a line of pine or spruce tree growing on a little dome of a mountain that rose above the treetops of our woods. Beyond the southeast corner of our fields were woods of oak and chestnut.

Spruce trees my father had planted surrounded the house, which stood back about six hundred feet from the main highway, facing north. The ground sloped away gently from it in all directions except the west side, where the slope was more pronounced and led to my great grandmother's lane (used as a public road in our time). We still walked to great grandmother's old well for our drinking water.

North of the house was a tall white pine, about two feet in diameter, grown from a little thing my Great Uncle Silas had brought on his shoulders from the woods. Just south of the house were three immense locust trees, the largest about three feet in diameter and seventy feet tall. When Uncle Silas was an old man of eighty-three and I a boy of five, he led me to this tree and told me it had been the same size when he was a boy.

It was a beautiful sight when these locust trees were loaded with their white blossoms, especially against black thunder clouds. They were like a painted picture, not a leaf or blossom stirring in the calm before the storm. Then, in the roar of the wind and thunder, the trees would sway and bend and the blossoms would fall like snow.

Locust trees in blossom

North of the house, across the driveway where stood the big stone mantle shelf from great grandmother's old house that was used as the horse block, there were three surviving trees of the old orchard, nearly a century old. One was a pear, leaning a bit and spindly at the top, but still loaded each year with delicious little pears. Hundreds of yellowjackets worked on those that fell to the ground. Often, if we picked up a pear to eat, we would find a yellowjacket eating its way in.

The other two trees were apples, the sturdier of which never bore fruit. The other, with partially-girdled trunk and only two live limbs, bore quantities of small, waxy red-and-yellow striped apples with sweet white pulp. Eventually, these old trees were broken off at their stumps by the weight of ice from sleet storms.

Further down the driveway, toward the west, was a

large elm and from there, running northward along the road to the main highway, was a row of beautiful maples. Still further west were a few more fruit trees, including one very old black cherry. This tree bore large cherries, but they were nearly always wormy, as we knew nothing of spraying in those days. A little south of the cherry tree, my father had planted eight or ten Bartlett and Sickle pear trees.

Also out near the highway was a group of apple trees, in addition to those we had in great variety in our orchard. There was a Tolman Sweeten, very old, fully forty feet high and more than twelve feet from the ground to the first limb. Large quantities of cider were made each year from its small, sweet fruit.

Apple varieties

A younger Tolman Sweeten and a Golden Russet yielded large, delicious apples. Other varieties were Baldwin, Greening, Snow. Maiden Blush, Northern Spy, King, Sourdough, Sheepnose (or Gillyflower), and one we called "Rattle Apple" because we could hear its seeds rattle.

Hickory nut trees—nineteen in all—were scattered about the property. A chestnut-timbered grape arbor, fifty feet long, was at the end of the lawn, south of the house. In season, it bore us a big crop of dusky blue Concord grapes. Between the arbor and the chestnut fence that bordered the lane in front of the barn buildings was a row of yellow pines, reaching to the end of the adjoining vegetable garden.

This garden was about fifty by a hundred feet. Near the row of pines was a long row of gooseberry bushes. North of them was the asparagus bed, with several Morris White peach trees near it. A long row of syringa bushes was between the peaches and a gravel path in the vegetable garden. Then came a patch of red and white poppies, a cherry tree, some pink rockets, a clump of ribbon grass, a sod path, a quince, some blue larkspur and a lilac. Beyond that was a large patch of

Our vegetable garden

red and white currant bushes at the north end of the garden. Between these and the sod path was the strawberry bed, covered with rye straw in winter, held down with bean poles.

There was no fence between the strawberry patch and the pasture, so cattle roaming about had knocked off the tops of the arbor vitae trees that surrounded the well.

In the vegetable garden were several kinds of tomatoes, pole beans, sweet corn and many other kinds of vegetables. Parsnips were left in the ground to freeze in winter, and celery was bleached by burying it in the dry earth of the cellar.

In summer, the house was surrounded with flowers. Across the road, west of the house, was a huge bed of white, pink and purple petunias, with a large clump of gray bouquet moss in the center. On the edge of this bed, my brother Robert had planted an elm tree.

Flowers

Along the driveway was a large oval flower bed of red and white geraniums. Down at the edge of the meadow were yellow marigolds and purple asters in a large, mounded bed. Pansies were thick in a long, narrow bed beside the horse block and near them coleus grew in a pink painted tub that was set on the stump of a long-gone hemlock.

In front of the porch was a small bed of dark red Jacquemont roses, with a large flower pot in the center which held our night-blooming cereus. Geraniums, a lilac, Bleeding Hearts, red and blue verbena, ribbon grass, sweet alyssum and portulacas grew in a large L-shaped bed east of the house. Sister Marion and I had our own small flower bed, and Robert had a Lily-of-the-Valley bed down by the crabapple tree.

In the middle of the large clover lawn south of the house was a bed of yellow Lady Slippers. At the northeast corner of this lawn, back of the house, was a row of arbor vitae, each fully sixteen feet high, making a sheltered spot for drying clothes. The main clothes-line extended south, past the crabapple, nearly to the grape arbor. The line was a solid galvanized iron wire, run through iron screw eyes on the post. Under the strain of the clothes in the wind, the wire working back and forth through the screw eyes made a peculiar grating squeak.

Drying wash in winter

In the winter, after Almira had done the washing, she would prepare herself for taking the basket of clothes outside to be hung. Tall and thin, she put Arctics on her feet, blue bed-ticking mittens on her hands, a gray shawl wound around her head and a checked gingham apron tied around her waist. It might be below zero with a gale blowing or light snow drifting. None of this stopped Almira.

With old-fashioned clothespins she worked back and forth, pinning big and little socks and what she called "so forths" till all the clothes were hung. They billowed in the wind and were frozen stiff by nightfall, when she carried them in, stacked like firewood.

Often, before a winter snowstorm, a flock of small snowbirds would perch on the clothesline before sheltering for the night. In spring and summer, an occasional robin or bluebird would rest on the line to watch the cats on the lawn below. At other times, we children used the line for a make-believe telegraph wire, tapping a code on it.

To the left of the path to the barn was the two-story cornhouse, built about 1864. On the ground floor were bins for storing ears of corn. Upstairs were bins for oats, rye, ground corn and buckwheat, as well as a carpenter shop.

On our way to the stables, we children would go past the cornhouse and look through a small crack between the wagon shed and the stable. The wagon shed had been built about 1812. In our time, it housed two square box wagons, an old buckboard, a spring wagon and some tools.

I was always careful to first look through the crack between the buildings to see if the old turkey gobbler who hated my red cravat was safely out of the way. If he was nowhere in sight, we would go into the stable to see the carriage horses, Fannie (named after my aunt) and Katie. Beyond the carriage stable was the stable for the farm's work horses, Gertrude, Jessie and others.

The old turkey gobbler

Connecting the two stables was a carriage house, also built in 1864. The yard for the horse stables was about fifty by seventy-five feet. An old ox cart stood in one corner, its edges worn smooth from animals scratching their necks on it.

The yard for the cow barn adjoined the stable yard, just east of it. A pine board fence, about seven feet high, separated the two yards, each surrounded by the fence, which had slat gates. We had a hundred or so white and brown Leghorn hens, some buff Cochins, Dominics and a Shanghai rooster. Their home was a two-story chicken house, just south of the wagon house. The chickens ran around the horse stable yard and under the gate into the cow barnyard to mingle with the cows.

Barns, coops and our "Big Barn"

All these animals got their water from a large round tub set in a break in the fence between the two yards and siphoned through a lead pipe which came from a hill a quarter of a mile away.

Separating the wagon shed and the cow barn was the "Big Barn," belonging to my great-grandmother's old place, built around 1785. Like the house, it was built of hewn timber, roofed with hand-riven shingles and nailed with hand-wrought nails. One of the white oak timbers, under the mow and over the thrashing floor, measured sixteen inches in diameter. The floor was of heavy oak planks, fastened with wooden pegs.

Originally, this barn had been painted Venetian red, but in later years had been re-sided with pine, which had become a weather-beaten gray. The barn doors were very large, with hinges that reached almost across them. At the bottom of the east door was little square opening we called the "cat hole."

Inside the barn the hay mow, straw mow and horse stalls faced the main floor, so that the animals could be fed from there, as was done in old-fashioned barns. On the threshing floor the sheep-shearing was done, the hay unloaded and the buckwheat and beans thrashed. In the barn we kept a pair of oxen, Damon and Pythias. On the other side of their enclosure was a calf pen.

Oxen and swallows

The barn's main bay took up two-thirds of the space and was full of timothy, red top and other kinds of hay. Up in the dark corners, inside the rafters, were mud swallow nests. We could see little blue feathers and yellow heads sticking out from them.

The swallows would fly down, swish past our faces and fly out the barn doors to enjoy the sky over our happy world, The Ridge.

"Mother's Toilet Table,"
a study from memory by Thomas Lossing.

Chapter III
CHILDHOOD MEMORIES AND
THANKSGIVING

When I was an infant, my mahogany crib stood in the southeast corner of my parents' bedroom. Its length filled the space between the corner and the nursery door. My younger sister, Marion, slept in the nursery.

The cream-colored bedroom wallpaper was decorated with light stripes and small red roses, both in bud and full bloom. I'm told I caused one of these buds—just above the crib—to come into full bloom by wetting my finger and rubbing it around and around.

Two pictures hung on the wall above the crib: a colored one of the Madonna and Child; the other a steel engraving of the Angel of the Sepulchre. A black walnut bracket hung near the picture of the Madonna and

25

held a blue leather New Testament (embossed with a gilt cross), a couple of other books and a pair of candy soldiers. Underneath the crib were two large drawers for blankets and other bedding.

The doors, baseboard and long wooden mantel of the bedroom were painted light green. White lace curtains, from ceiling to floor, hung over the windows. A brown carpet covered the floor.

My parents' wide oak bed backed up to the north wall of the room. It was covered with a white spread, pillow and bolster with a sham. Near the corner, on the east side of the room, stood a tall oak bureau. Into a red jar on the bureau my mother put her "snarls," which would later be made into puffs. Beside the bureau, a door opened into the room of my older sister, Penelope.

Blankets and pin cushions

Opposite the bed, on the south side of the room, stood my mother's toilet table, between two windows. It was a large, waist-high cedar chest, with a top that opened. A till at one end held odds and ends of dress goods. The rest of it was filled with large pink blankets with blue and white stripes at the ends. These had been woven in my uncle's woolen mills. The drawer at the bottom of the toilet table held a blue and white homespun counterpane and an extra set of lace curtains.

The top of the toilet table was covered with a brown linen scarf. In the center of it was set a red pin cushion, about ten inches square. In this were stuck common pins, safety pins, needles—threaded and unthreaded—and some slim, black-headed hat pins. We children thought it fun to squeeze the pin cushion to see how many pins and needles would pop out. At one side of the pin cushion was a tall glass decanter with a glass stopper. This decanter must have held very common cologne, for we were allowed free access to it and Mother always laughed when she smelled it on us.

A pair of black-lacquered, square Japanese tea

boxes—with hinges broken and smelling of tinfoil—were all my father had to show for co-signing a tradesman's note for $1,500. One of these boxes stood at each end of the toilet table. When I was still very young, I would drag a chair to the toilet table, climb on to it, open the right-hand tea box, reach far down inside and come up with a handful of puffy egg crackers and thin oatmeal cookies.

This feast, often moistened with water sucked through a baby bottle, was sometimes consumed on the back of Billy, an old wooden hobby horse, which I could mount only with the aid of a chair for a horse block.

My rocking horse, "Billy"

Billy's side, made of calfskin, was badly moth-eaten, but his mouth and nostrils were as red as if they were new. One of his green glass eyes had been broken by brother Robert, but the one that remained seemed mild and kindly to me. Billy's brush of a cow tail was apt to be most anywhere, but his leather bridle and his red saddle were held in place by brass-headed nails.

The contents of the left-hand tea box were always controlled by Mother. I, being one subject to croup, knew the box contained a bottle of ipecac. At the faintest sound of a croupy cough in the night, I would hear the rattle of the tea box cover, followed by Mother's whisper, "Here, dear, take this," and she would rub ipecac on my lips.

Sharing the left-hand tea box with the ipecac were china salve boxes full of mutton tallow for greasing chapped hands and noses. After she greased our hands, Mother would enclose them in square, thumbless Canton flannel bags. When we tried to scratch or pull up a blanket, our hands felt to us more like webbed feet than hands.

At bedtime I would repeat the Lord's Prayer after my mother. I could usually hear my little sister in the nursery repeating after Father, "Now I lay me down to sleep,

Bedtime

27

I pray the lord my soul to keep." At that age, I found the word "soul" confusing, for I always associated it with the sole of my mother's slipper.

After Marion said her prayers, father would walk the floor with her in his arms, humming her to sleep with one or the other of his two tunes, "Yankee Doodle" or the Doxology. Mother rocked me to sleep in her yellow rocking chair by the window, singing to me, or telling me Bible stories. Often she would sing,

> Once upon a time there were three bears
> that lived in the woods,
> One was a huge bear ...

I pressed my hand under her chin to feel the vibration of her singing, and if I noticed her voice trailing off into drowsiness, would command her to "Sing!" She might then get as far as "The wee little bear ..." but I was likely not to know for I would have fallen fast asleep.

A dream of Heaven

One bright, moonlit night, when mother was rocking me and telling me a Bible story, I looked out the window and saw our three great locust trees swaying and bending in the strong west wind. The way to Heaven in the stars above, I decided, must be up through the largest of the locust trees.

That night I dreamed I began to climb that tree on my way to Heaven. At the top of the tree I had to climb up a long, heavy stepladder, and at the top of the ladder I had to go through a scuttle hole. Then, there I was, in Heaven!

Heaven seemed all aglow, a bright gold glow. Sitting on a stool was the Lord, looking exactly like the steel engraving of the Guardian Angel that hung above my crib. At the Lord's right hand was a tall blue cupboard, full of materials for making rag dolls. The Lord was making one. He looked up, saw me—and there my dream ended!

The bedroom was a cozy place in the daytime, especially when the sun poured in. Tiger, our big gray-striped cat, dozed in the red Boston rocker by the window.

Tiger would not flick an ear at our romping game in which we used my crib for a haymow, but let a chimney swallow swoop down the flue to its nest, and Tiger would be there in a leap. With one forepaw raised, he would crane his head way up inside the chimney, wishing he could catch the bird which was out of reach.

Tiger the cat

At night, weird shadows filled the room as the tiny flicker from the night light in the hall fell on garments flung over the back of a chair, or on father's wooden bootjack on the hearth, or on the dried grasses on the mantel. Chimney swallows rumbled in the flue. Outside, on a snowbank, Hawkeye, our shepherd, howled at the moon. And I was safely tucked in my crib.

My Uncle Robert and Aunt Fannie Titus's family and ours consisted of six members each: ours with two girls and two boys, my uncle's with one boy and three girls. Our Thanksgivings were always spent together, although we lived nineteen miles apart, which meant at that season of the year a long ride over rough, frozen roads. We alternated between the two places.

Thanksgiving with our cousins

About eleven o'clock on Thanksgiving Day, our joy was immense as we waited for the company. By then, with our spy glass, we could catch a glimpse of them coming over Cole's hill more than two miles away. It was always a great thrill to see their wagon. My uncle drove a large three-seated spring wagon with a top, curtains hanging down the sides. Then came the suspense of, perhaps, half an hour or more until we could see them again, this time easily without the glass.

They would be coming along the piece of road in front of the cheese factory. Then we had a wait of perhaps fifteen minutes after which they would appear again as they came to the top of O'Brien's hill, less than a quarter of a mile away. By this time we young ones couldn't stand still at all. There were squeals of delight and even old Hawkeye knew something was up.

My father and mother, dressed in their best—mother with ruching in her neck and lacy cuffs turned back over her sleeves—were ready to go to the door. The visitors would be turning into the driveway and, as they approached the horse block, we all rushed out to meet them, my sisters in their best woolen dresses and clean white aprons, I with a little blue suit.

The Titus family arrives

In the front seat were my uncle and Cousin Helen (my favorite and my age), she wearing a yellow overcoat with a cape and her red-mittened hands laid out on the buffalo robe. My uncle, with his fur mittens, got out on the horse block and unbuttoned the side curtains. The horses, steaming and sweating, were glad to stand after the long journey. One by one the rest of the Titus family came out, first the children, then Aunt Fannie—my mother's sister. They were like creatures from the ark, it seemed to us. Last of all came Ann, their fat, colored nurse who was of the old type, with a blue plaid turban on her head.

As soon as all the wraps were removed there was a whisper at the dining room door and my mother immediately responded, then came back into the parlor to announce that dinner was ready. All would be laughing and chattering in happy expectation. Uncle Robert was a witty man and my father and he exchanged compliments.

The great roaring fire in the fireplace snapped and, before leaving to go into the dining room, a brass-mounted fender that had belonged to my great grandmother was placed in front of the fire. As we came through the door we would see the long table, set with the best white china dishes, silver knives with ivory handles, large cut-glass goblets, the immense soup tureen that had also belonged to my great grandmother, with reddish-brown pagoda pattern, and beside it the big silver ladle.

The twelve of us seated ourselves, my mother in a tall, straight, fiddle-backed chair, like many others of its time, supposed to have been sat in by George Washington. She would ask the blessing. Through the silent blessing, we young ones would fidget.

The dinner

The arrival of the turkey on its huge platter, brought in by Esther, our colored maid, and placed in front of my father, was the cause for much smiling. The carving was almost a perpetual task as plates were passed back and forth for second helpings. Jolly stories, with a flavor of history, were told by my father, and the year's events recounted as we ate the turkey, cranberries, boiled onions, mashed potatoes, Hubbard squash or beets, home-made bread and butter.

Then came the big plum pudding that had caused so much anxiety in its preparation but never failed perfection, and its accompanying wine sauce. Last came hickory nuts from our own trees, already cracked and served in a large vegetable dish which belonged to the same set as the soup tureen of my great grandmother's. This would be passed around and each person had a nut pick with an ivory handle.

While the grown folks were talking, we young ones were eating immense quantities of delicious food and grinning at each other in anticipation of the games after dinner.

Then came the games! Puss-in-the-corner was played out in the hall, and hide-and-seek all over the house. Later followed the more quiet games of parchesi and the checker-game-of-life, played by shaking dice for the number of squares to move. If we had to move on the square that said "marry," we would look blinky; if on the square that said "go to jail," cousin Helen would

Our games

kick up her heels with joy, especially if I drew it. There were other squares that represented a good occupation or pleasant sports, such as "coasting" and "cricket," and these were the coveted ones.

Thanksgiving evening

In spite of all that we had to eat at Thanksgiving dinner, our active games, played into late afternoon, gave us a feeling of hunger, and we began to think of supper with considerable eagerness. Alas, supper on Thanksgiving night consisted only of light sandwiches at six o'clock and chocolate and fruitcake passed around in the parlor by Esther, who brought in the big tin, oval trays. The food was served on china plates mother had painted from her own designs.

These supper plates were white with a dainty wreath of green leaves, blue and pink starry blossoms around the edges and a sprig of blossoms in the center. There were cups and saucers to match. Mother poured the chocolate from a pitcher which had been given by her father, who also gave its duplicate to Aunt Fannie. The pitcher was of distinctive design, made especially for the two sisters. When it sat on its silver tray, gleaming in the firelight, it was a beautiful thing.

Our parlor

At the south of the room was a square Steinway piano, with a kerosene student lamp on the left corner. On this piano, Miriam, at eight years of age, played Beethoven's concertos, to the great admiration of Professor Ritter of the music department of Vassar College. Near the piano was the door to the dining room and near this door was a mahogany card table, its polished top open against the wall. At the other end of the piano was a round wicker table, about two feet in diameter and quite high, on an elaborate wicker base mounted on castors. Upon it and resting on the thick, dark red, round table mat, was a large seashell of rainbow colors, filled with water in which were red geraniums picked fresh from Mother's greenroom.

Nearby was a small wicker chair that once had been

a high chair for my mother when she was a little girl, but which had had its legs sawed off to make it of ordinary height. Back of this table and chair, and against the wall, was a long black walnut screen about four feet high and eight long, of solid wood with a graceful, conventional design cut through the wood, making an open-work pattern. Hanging over the screen was a painting of a mountain stream in the Adirondacks, framed in black walnut.

At the end of the screen was the southeast corner of the room, a space between this corner and the fireplace was taken up by two chairs and the east window. This window and the two north windows were curtained with very heavy crimson silk, lined with white, which hung sweeping to the floor from a gilt frame at the ceiling. The silk was handsomely brocaded in a flower design.

Curtains, fireplace and floors

Beside each of these windows stood a mahogany chair with a high back, designed by my mother, and the seats were upholstered with a patterned silk to match the curtains. Under all the windows, when the curtains were parted, showed a wooden panel painted a warm gray. The ceiling was white, the walls of the room papered with gilt-striped paper. The chimney-well projected into the room about three feet and contained a large fireplace with brass andirons and fender which had belonged to my great grandmother. The opening of this fireplace was trimmed with gray Irish marble, which was encased with a high colonial mantel of white pine, painted to match the room.

At the right of the room was a straight-backed chair, a fiddle-back originally belonging to my great grandmother. The floor was covered with light-colored matting and in front of the fire was a plush rug in red and blue. Under one of the north windows was a white angora rug, and other smaller rugs were scattered about the room. At the left of the fireplace and in front of the chimney was a dome of white coral from the West Indies, which we young ones used to look at and think wonderful. Beside the coral stood the fire tools with brass handles.

On the mantle, on each corner, stood a candelabra of iron, gilded, holding three candles. It had a base of white marble and long pendants of cut glass hung from each candle socket. (When the morning sun shone through the open east window it threw dancing spots of iridescent light in different parts of the room as the pendants swayed with the morning breeze).

Next to the candelabra on the mantel were iridescent globes of glass for holding flowers. In the center of the chimney piece hung a picture of the Madonna and Child. On each side of the mantel, on the fluted pilasters, hung a plaque made by Indians from a small deer's foot, embodying the cloven hoof and about eight inches of the skin, flattened out, with two dark blue pockets sewed on the front of the skins. These pockets were beautifully encrusted with blue, red and white beads. Each plaque was suspended by a small chain of the same sort of beads hung over a brass hook.

Glass and plaques in the parlor

Between the corner of the fireplace and the northeast corner of the room stood a chest of drawers, made of a heavy, dark, unidentified wood, which had been given us by Aunt Elizabeth Sweet, who told us that it was over two hundred years old and had come from our ancestors on Long Island. On this chest of drawers stood a tall vase of wood and glass, designed by my mother. The drawers were full of photographs from Turkey. In the corner by the chest was a silk American flag and staff, which had been carried in Poughkeepsie when the 150th Regiment was leaving for Gettysburg. On the other side of the chest was a blue banner with gold lace trimming and a design worked in by my mother and sister and considered ornamental to our parlor.

Between the two windows on the north side stood a marbletop table with bulging mahogany feet and castors. The table never stood exactly level on account of its heavy top. In the center of this table was a high bronze sperm-oil lamp with a round, ground glass globe, encircling a glass chimney. I never saw this lamp lighted. Also on the table was a little set of gilt reindeer, dragging a small, fancy wagon, not unlike an old-fashioned fire engine, but where the boiler would be was a perfumery container. This whole thing was mounted on a white marble base.

Keepsakes and some novelties

Also on this table was a little bronze whale, about six inches long, mounted on a pedestal, carrying a bronze man on its back—a really beautifully fashioned article. There was also a wooden manikin on the table, a ferocious-looking creature, with wooden whiskers and with white beads having black centers for eyes that were set deep in his head. The Swiss man who had fashioned this had made it so the head could be pulled out of his neck and used as a letter seal. Each leg could be pulled out in the same manner—one used for a pencil, the other for a pen. One arm could be used as a small knife for sharpening a pencil. By lifting the whole manikin off the base, an ink bottle was uncovered.

Beside this manikin was a small, round plaid box with a glass cover which showed two wiggly imitation turtles, a relic of the Philadelphia Centennial. In front of the table stood another high-backed chair, very much of the same design as the one near the fireplace. In the northwest corner was a round table with a dark, India-red cloth on it. In its center was another student lamp and a few books and photographs of family and scenery.

A photograph of Swiss peasants was on the table, in a scroll frame of black walnut. It had been given to my father and mother as a Christmas present by its maker, a Swiss workman named John Sheis, who had lived on our place. Another thing on this table was an inlaid box containing some relics from the West Indies, a part of the Rock of Gibraltar and a dunce cap made of coconut fiber. Between this corner table and the door which opened into the hall was one more of the mahogany chairs like those by the windows.

Everything in the room had been thoroughly examined many and many a time. My father had a great collection of curios with which we were all familiar. It was a most wonderful setting for a game of "hide the thimble" and my father would sit there talking with the elders, seemingly unaware of what we were doing, but very often he would secretly point out the hiding place to us younger children who were seeking the thimble.

Finding thimbles

It was fully dark when my father went with my uncle to harness the horses for the Titus family's return journey that evening. We younger ones were too sleepy to respond to the "good nights," and after the departure of our guests we went off to bed, drowsily happy and unaware that we were storing up reminiscences for years to come.

A view of Poughkeepsie from across the Hudson,
by Benson Lossing

Chapter IV
PEDDLERS, ORGAN-GRINDERS
AND CHARACTERS

When spring opened and the roads improved, Honest
John, the tin peddler, was sure to drive in with his high,
enclosed red wagon.

Honest John

This wagon had doors on the side and at the end
which he could raise to show his tinware. These included dippers of all sizes, tea kettles with copper
bottoms, colanders, flour sifters, big and little milk
pans, six- to ten-quart pails, and a variety of colored
suspenders. Honest John would sell for cash or trade
for scrap iron.

He would look over your pile of iron, estimate its
weight, and offer his "very highest price," which would
be a mere nothing. I found out it was a great deal bet-

37

ter to weigh the iron than to trust Honest John's judgment. A big team with a spring wagon would come later to pick up the iron traded in for tinware. I once traded him a cookstove for a pair of suspenders, which were worth more to me.

Honest John's wagon, horses and wares really belonged to a man who owned an iron foundry as well as a tin shop in a neighboring town. Honest John was quite short, bow-legged and middle-aged. He had driven this wagon for years, and his stock was always in good order. He almost never spoke. He would show his tinware but would never praise it nor coax one to buy.

A sure sign of spring

Seeing Honest John's wagon was a sure sign of spring, for he appeared just as regularly as the bluebirds and robins. To me, his arrival was one of the main events of the year, like the circus, for what could be gayer than the big, red-bodied wagon with yellow wheels and a jet black horse, Honest John riding upon his high seat?

As soon as any one of us spied him coming in the distance the word would be passed along and we would all rush out. We would already have our piles of scrap iron, consisting of worn-out horseshoes, barrel hoops, wagon tires, broken axles and plow shares, broken mold boards (the part of a plow that turns the sod), old stoves, broken three-legged iron pots and worn out parts of mowing machines.

Another sign of spring was the sound of a fish horn from a peddler bringing Hudson River shad. He drove a skinny, old horse attached to a square wagon with a butcher cart box in the back, usually dripping water from the ice. He would brace the lid when he raised it, and hung the scales to it to weigh the fish. After weighing the fish he cut off the head and threw it in the grass where it would be grabbed immediately by a cat who had been waiting for just that gift. She would chew on it and growl at the peddler while he was scaling and cleaning the fish.

Most of these itinerant peddlers were too old and decrepit to do anything else. One exception to the elderly fish peddlers was a small boy who lived near the Hudson and whose father had given him a team of Shetland ponies and a small square box wagon to fit. Of his own accord, the boy went to peddling shad in and about Poughkeepsie and did very well, as people liked the cute outfit.

Instead of the rising sun coming over the hill, it might be the round-faced, "palm-leaf" pack peddler, so-called because he always carried a large palm-leaf fan. He wore a broad-brimmed, straw hat tied with a cord under his chin.

The "palm-leaf" pack peddler

He had a flat, blue-eyed face, benign in expression, and was short and stocky, carrying an immense, brown denim-covered pack on his back. In one hand he held a long staff and in the other the palm leaf fan. His whole appearance was neat and clean. He was known all over the county for the dress goods and laces that he brought and for his reliability and his simple mind.

His walk was deliberate as he approached the back door. None of the dogs barked at him as he unstrapped his pack and spread out his calicoes and other goods on the porch. He showed all his goods, perhaps making a sale to the two girls in the kitchen, then strapped up his pack and left with a bow, having uttered scarcely a word.

Unlike the "palm-leaf" peddler was one who had called at my grandfather's house in Poughkeepsie years before and sold my grandmother a bolt of "beautiful silk," which he unrolled for a couple of yards for her inspection. After he left, my grandmother unrolled the bolt a little more and found the remainder to be only cheap cotton goods. My grandfather immediately ran after the peddler, overtaking him down the street. He grabbed him by the shoulders and kicked him the three blocks to the courthouse where the peddler was made to reimburse my grandfather—and my grandfather was made to pay forty dollars to the court for kicking the peddler!

He always said it was worth it.

Hartwell's butcher cart

Twice a week, at about eleven o'clock, we heard the bell of Mr. Hartwell's butcher cart. My father always rushed down from his study to select the meat, but Hawkeye, our shepherd dog, would always be there before him. Hawkeye knew the sound of the horse's feet and wanted to be sure of his bone.

As a rule, we young ones ran to the cart as soon as we heard the bell, and I can remember yet the sound of the meat saw and the cleaver wielded by the rosy-faced Mr. Hartwell. I can still see him in his long white apron, with deep straw cuffs, as he rolled up a roast and pushed the skewers in to hold it.

On a shelf in the top of the cart's body were the cleaver, saw, knives, steel sharp, and the bell. On the lid of the cart hung the scales. (Fine steaks were twelve to sixteen cents a pound, pot roasts nine.) In hot weather, this meat was wrapped up and let down in buckets to the water's edge of our deep well to stay cool.

Mrs. Garvey

The first appearance of Mrs. Garvey was at our front door on a winter's day. There was snow on the ground and she seemed dressed in innumerable layers of clothes, cowhide shoes, white stockings, a heavy dark green shawl on her broad shoulders and a quilted brown hood framing her middle-aged, strong, mountain face. On her arm she carried a square market basket.

As my mother opened the door, our caller looked at

her out of honest, round, blue eyes and said in a strong voice: "I'm Mrs. Garvey, and I'm peddlin' salve." My mother invited her into the library, where there was a good warm fire, and Mrs. Garvey exclaimed in awe at the number of books she saw about her. Balls of snow stuck to her heels gradually melted and ran out on the oak floor as she sat in a straight-backed chair. She often reached down to the basket at her side, taking out small, round boxes of salve.

This salve, she described as being good for rheumatism, backache, muscle strain, sore throat, chilblains, frostbite, chapped and cracked hands and stiff neck. "There warn't nothing but yarbs in it," she assured us, because she had made it herself and, with a smile of cunning, she added, "Of course I ain't a-tellin' what they be."

Her salve for aches

We bought several of the ten-cent boxes and she was "much obliged" for the sale. She said the death of her husband was the reason for having to peddle salve. She mentioned she was a sister-in-law to Mrs. Murphy who lived about a mile and a half down the road. During the Civil War, Mrs. Murphy's husband had been shot at the Battle of Gettysburg, and Mrs. Garvey's husband had caught him in his arms, where he died.

During this dramatic description, Mrs. Garvey sat waving her hands and rolling her eyes, giving us a pattern for our future amateur theatricals when we would dress up like her, white stockings and all, and go through the whole scene.

With a, "Well I must go," she departed abruptly.

On some spring mornings unfamiliar music could be heard, and upon going out to investigate we would find the Italian organ grinder turning the crank of his box-like organ that rested on its one leg. His monkey would be crawling around, fastened on a leash secured outside its little red coat, holding a tin cup and grimacing

The organ grinder

from under its red cap. Spring appeared to draw these organ grinders out from the city. It seemed to us to be quite like being out in the world to hear them, and it would remind us of New York, delighting us to be near such a strange creature as the monkey.

One little monkey was taught to fire a toy gun that exploded a paper cap and made a noise like a small torpedo. But it was an ordeal for him as he danced with excitement on his hind legs and held the gun at arm's length, his head turned away and eyes shut until he finally pulled the trigger. Then he threw down the gun and seemed immensely relieved.

The organ grinder's monkey

After the organ grinder finished playing several tunes, the monkey passed his cup. The man soon took off his hat, made a sweeping bow, shouldered his organ and monkey and traveled on.

The mailman John Wing

John Wing used to carry the mail from Dover to the Chestnut Ridge post office, a five-mile trip one way, a total of ten miles on foot, six days a week, the year round, through rain and snow and zero weather.

Tall and bony, Mr. Wing wore an ordinary suit, a black overcoat, a black slouch hat and, in a snowstorm, would have a gray, knitted scarf tied over his hat and wrapped around his neck, then tucked into his coat. He wore leather boots in the winter, greased with mutton tallow and lampblack. His trousers were outside his boots and, in snowy weather, were tied tightly around his ankles with heavy string. He had narrow, brown chin-whiskers, streaked with gray and wore a brown wig of quite long hair. His brown eyes squinted from a nervous affliction, and his nose was rather aquiline.

On his route, Mr. Wing left Dover Plains, turning through the entrance to a pasture, walking across this pasture and up the hill until he struck a steep pitch, called the "cart road." He followed this road through the woods, down a private grass-grown road and across a log bridge. He went through a gate, up a long lane, over a fence, on a continual rise, across a rolling field to the lot belonging to Mrs. Murphy, then out onto the main road.

He followed the main road until the corner of our meadow, near the hickory tree and the red gate. Across this meadow was his winding, beaten path to our driveway. The rest of his route was from our house down through the orchard and through O'Brien's woods, out through Mary Shelley's lane to the road and on to the Chestnut Ridge post office at Ann Wing's.

Mr. Wing carried a heavy leather mailbag and a small leather bag for my father's mail. Both bags were sweatstained and often bulged with packages. For years he held this mail route, only occasionally sending a substitute. His gait was so stiff that one would swear he had two wooden legs. He never smiled but always made some pleasant remark to us.

The bone picker was a Civil War veteran of about sixty who drove a skinny old horse attached to a square box wagon, going around the country picking up bones of all descriptions, which he took to a dealer in the town. There they were placed in a large bin until there was enough for a carload, then were shipped away to a fertilizer factory.

The old bone picker

This old bone picker was crippled in one leg and his back, and he carried a very crooked cane that looked like the root of a tree. It took him a long time to get out of his wagon. He was tall and gaunt, with bushy brown whiskers, and he evidently had not washed for years. His lower eyelids sagged, he had a high-bridged nose, the skin on his face was in ridges, and his complexion was like a dried-up raisin. The back of his neck lay in creases full of dirt. His arms were long and ape-like.

In one hand he carried a sack to put old bones in,

and in the other had the crooked cane. In this manner he would start out to gather up bones around the houses, barns and chicken yards of the farms. When he saw a bone, he would bend over, pick it up, and put it in his bag, then always said in his very deep voice, "Bah!" evidently an exclamation of pain that came every time he straightened up.

If a bone happened to be in a hole, he would scratch around with his cane until he got it where he could pick it up, then maybe he would look at you out of his saggy eyes and say, "Bah!" again.

He lived alone in Oniontown. One day I saw him purchasing a candle in the country store there. He hobbled in and hung his cane on the edge of the counter as he fumbled for a dime. He laid the dime on the counter with a groan, and hoarsely demanded, "Gimme one candle." When the clerk wrapped it up and gave it to him, he said, "Bully boy with the glass eye!" and hobbled out again.

His funeral

When the old bone picker died, he had the largest attendance at his funeral I had ever seen. The procession of wagons was at least an eighth of a mile long. It was a Masonic funeral from the Baptist Church. The Masons were dressed in their full regalia.

Ore-bed Amy

Through the woods in the section where we lived were holes two or three feet deep and from two to six feet in diameter. These all were dug by "Ore-bed Amy," a man who had owned considerable property but had lost it. The loss had affected his mind and forever afterward he was looking for iron ore. He always asked permission to dig the ore and it was never refused him. The holes in the rough woods caused no one any inconvenience.

Ore-bed Amy was a man of sixty, smooth-shaven, not very large. He usually wore a Prince Albert coat and a black slouch hat and always appeared neat.

Once, when he was standing on a box preaching the Gospel, some boys set fire to his coattails, and all he said as he doubled up and smothered it out was, "Don't, boys, don't," and then kept right on preaching.

Ore-bed Amy carried with him pictures illustrating what he claimed was an invention of his for grinding mowing machine knives. The illustration showed him turning the grinding machine with his foot and holding a long set of knives on the stone. We came into possession of one of these machines, and it proved to be not one half as good as an ordinary grindstone.

These, and others like them, came over our road to The Ridge. They were part of our lives year after year, and we eagerly looked forward to their visits. We welcomed those who arrived unexpectedly and not according to schedule (like the regular visits of the butcher and some tradespeople) and great was our disappointment if we discovered that such a visitor had been along and, for some reason, we had missed him.

Shantynette Wheeler was justice of the peace and lived along the road by the grist mill near the Connecticut line. He used to drink quite a lot. His nose was a perfect blossom and he had a temper to go with it.

Shantynette Wheeler, justice of the peace

At one time Shantynette got into some financial trouble, so he placed his property into the hands of his brother, Theodore. When his trouble was over, he wanted his property back, but Theodore would not give it to him, claiming he would drink it all up, and that it would be better to give him what he needed through his life.

One day, about one o'clock in the morning, a couple came down from the East Mountain to be married by the justice of the peace. Shantynette came to the window in his nightcap, threw open the sash, and called out, "I pronounce you man and wife!"

Gil Denny

Gilbert Denny—"Gil"—owned a portable sawmill. He would purchase, fell the trees and saw them into railroad ties. As a youth, I used to go over the felled trees with him, estimating the number of ties each would produce.

One evening I went up to see him. Mrs. Denny ushered me in and said she expected her husband back at any minute. The room was hot and stuffy, but Mrs. Denny wore a green shawl over her head as she stirred something on the stove. After commenting on the weather for a few minutes, she told me that Gil and she had had a pretty bad winter and now the family were all down with the mumps. I said, "He'll be tired when he gets home, so I'll come back later."

I recall thinking, as soon as I got outside, that somehow Gil would do all right. He was a very ordinary-looking man, but of superior intelligence and he had a way of hiring help for very little money. I was always of the opinion that he had made quite a lot of money, despite the fact he and his family lived in a typical mountain home.

Bens Denny

Gil's brother, Bens, was much older. He was a large man, with bushy brown whiskers, an aquiline nose and small, brown, deep-set eyes. He was in the logging and sawmill business long before Gil, but seemed to show much less business judgment. His mill was too large. It cost too much to move around and, instead of buying just the timber on a tract, he would buy the land itself. The result was that he paid taxes for years on unproductive woodland which had been lumbered off soon after he had purchased it.

Years before, Bens had started to build a large house on his land in the valley, but lack of money or something else kept him from completing it, so he continued to live in the little house which had no windows and was painted only with a white primer coat.

Bens was quite superstitious. For instance, he would start out in the morning to look at a tract of timber. If a red squirrel ran across the road, it was a sign of bad luck and he would leave his mission for another day.

One time, I asked him to come and saw a piece of old chestnut timber for us. He said he would as soon as he finished sawing where he was. He kept promising for weeks and weeks that he would finish the last five logs of the job he was working on, then come to our place to do our sawing. He complained of being ill so, finally, I said I would steam up his sawmill, saw his five logs and then move the mill for him to our place. He readily agreed.

Bens's sawmill

The mill outfit weighed over twelve tons. To lighten the load, we took off the engine which was mounted on the steam boiler. With the aid of a six-horse team, we finally got the mill to its new location. Ben still complained of being ill and seemed to have lost all interest in the job at hand. He suggested I use the mill and saw my piece of timber, with no charge for the use of the mill, provided I return it to his home, down in the valley.

I proceeded to saw the piece I wanted. Before we moved the mill back to Bens's place, the Brothers of Nazareth asked if they could bring over some custom logs for milling. On the appointed day, we steamed up the mill but the promised logs never came. We then faced the task of dismantling the mill and returning it to Bens, when word came that he was dead. After that, the mill stood rusting in the woods, awaiting word from his executors. One day it was missing and I learned that the party who held a mortgage on it had taken it—to my great relief, for that meant I would not have to move it.

Down at what we called the Red Gate of our place (which was at the turn of the road leading to a meadow)

47

there was an immense old hollow log covered with wild raspberry bushes. Discovered in this log one day was an old man in a greatly weakened condition, talking deliriously about his gold spectacles.

Jim Rossel, a nearby farmer, took him a basket of food, but before the old man could rally sufficiently to eat it, he died. The authorities were notified and it was learned that he had wandered sometime before from the County House. To us youngsters, the old log was evermore considered haunted and none dared set foot in it. We would make quick, darting visits to look at it, but always in broad daylight.

From our dining room window at night we could see, on far off Thomassteene Mountain, a light that seemed as bright as a lighthouse. It was the kitchen lamp of Jim Rossel. His window panes were kept so clean, the lamp chimney so bright and the wick so neatly trimmed that Jim Rossel's light was known all over the community.

Jim Rossel was a handy man when it came to helping shingle a barn, making a sled or shearing sheep. He had a leach barrel containing wood ashes for making lye for soap, which was customary in many of these old places. He drove an old gray horse hitched to a buckboard, and when going to work as carpenter, he carried his tool chest in the back of the wagon. This chest was very large, but had hardly anything in it, except a broadaxe and chalk line.

Short and fat, Jim had scrubby chin whiskers from ear to ear. His favorite phrase was "By Jipinetty!" When he'd finish shingling a roof, he'd bellow, "By Jipinetty it won't leak!" Jim was well liked. Living with him was his daughter, Sarah (always called "Sairy"), a maiden lady of thirty who was short like her father and must have weighed more than two hundred pounds. She had blue eyes, a putty-like complexion, wore white stockings and had big feet. She later married Alvie Allen and moved to the Hollow to live there with him. She continued the tradition of "Jim Rossel's Lamp," always setting one in the window of her new home, as bright as ever.

On account of its location, however, it could not be seen for any great distance, as Jim's had been.

His house was one of the typical eighteen-by-twenty-foot houses built in that section years before. Many an old foundation, overgrown with moss, could be found in the woods, sometimes with a lilac bush or old apple tree nearby, among the oaks and chestnuts. After Jim died, his house was unoccupied and gradually decayed.

A lamp in the window

*Benson Lossing's sketch of Henry Van Meter,
an elderly black man.*

Chapter V
COLORED HELP AND NEIGHBORS

About two o'clock one winter afternoon, when it was snowing a few flakes, I heard a knock on the kitchen door, and when I opened it there stood about four feet of colored boy in a pair of Number Ten German leather boots.

He wore a cap of brown plush, with a gray squirrel's tail sewed across the front of it, ear flaps tied securely under his chin. His tired eyes looked up from under the cap as he said to me, "Do you want to hire a man?"

His faded blue overcoat was neatly mended, and beneath it showed the usual blue jacket buttoned up to his chin. His blue and white homemade bedticking mittens had their thumbs thrust in his overcoat pock-

*Edward
Bradford*

51

ets. His large boots had no heels, so he stood at a peculiar angle.

As we had only a few days before decided we would not hire any more colored boys, my answer to this newcomer's question was in the negative. Then he asked if he might come and get warm, and of course that privilege was given him. I placed him in a chair on the brick hearth near the stove, where he gradually thawed out and removed his hat and coat. The snow on his boots melted into a puddle on the bricks, but still he sat.

After a while my mother asked his name. He said it was Edward Bradford and that he was twelve years old. To the question, "Where did you come from?" he replied, "Below Ann Wing's, toward Clove Hollow." It was now after lunchtime, but Mother fixed him up with a plate of food on a side table.

The storm was by this time increasing, and Mother said, "As the days are so short, Edward, don't you think you had better start back to Ann Wing's?"

He squirmed around in his chair, gazed out of the window, and said, "I never leave a place after snow fly."

So what could we do? This Edward stayed two years! He was the best helper there ever was, and never expected any reward beyond his clothes and a bit of pin money. He was immaculate with his clothes, did his own mending, and made his own mittens, which accounted for his neat appearance upon his arrival.

Morris

Morris came with the team of black horses—Fannie and Katie—that we purchased from my uncle.

My uncle always paid the Dutchess Turnpike toll gate charges by the year, and after we purchased the team Morris kept driving through the toll gate without the gate keeper being advised of the change in ownership. Consequently, the charges were made to my uncle, and

Morris thought he had done a smart, cunning thing. But eventually my father had to fix it up with my uncle and reprimand Morris.

Then there were Jacob, Almira and Gertrude.

Jacob was our gardener and cared for the horses. He drove for my father and his wife, Almira, was cook. They were both splendid and sensible, tall and slender and very dark.

Jacob, Almira and Gertrude

Jacob had fought with the Northern troops in the Civil War, and following a head wound had had a silver plate inserted under his scalp. I remember their child, Gertrude, when she was about seven years old and always with a ready laugh. In the early morning hours her hair was done up with white curl papers, and she usually wore a green gingham apron.

We were told by our mother what hours we could play out with the colored children on the place. We would play tag, and it was such fun to hear Gertrude's rippling laughter. Her cheeks were just like chipmunk's.

We would play a game, as Gertrude danced up to one of us and sang:

> Here we go up the green grass, green grass, green grass,
> Here we go up the green grass on a dusty, dusty day.
> Will you come out? No, Paddy me oh, she won't come out,
> She won't come out, Paddy me oh, She won't come out this dusty, dusty day.

Then Gertrude would dance up to another member of the group and say, "Will you come out?" and we'd sing:

> Yes, Paddy me oh, she will come out,

She will come out, Paddy me oh. She will come
out on this dusty, dusty day.
You will have a chance, my dear, you will have
another,
The bells are ringing, we all sing now
And clap our hands together.

Then we all joined hands and circled around the one
in the center, singing:

Paddy me oh, she will come out.

The hour for playing in the house was between four
and six. One of our favorite games for then was "Poison," a game invented by ourselves.

We played by taking magazines and papers and plac-
ing them at distances as far as we could step apart.
Our route started in the library, around the library table,
taking in any stray rug for islands, out through the door
and down the hall, into the dining room and around
the long dining table, then back to the library again.

We would all rush as fast as we could from one paper to another. Whoever missed and stepped on the
floor was "poisoned."

Blackboard for a slide

Another favorite game for this hour of play indoors
was to turn our father's black walnut stepladder over
on its face and place a blackboard on its slanting legs.
Then we would climb up on a chair and slide down
the blackboard out onto the solid oak floor of the library. The blackboard became as shiny as could be
on the back, except where it was scarred by children's
buttons.

As a sideshow one evening I was tipping Gertrude
over backwards in a straight-backed rocking chair and
gently let the back of the chair rest on the floor. This I
repeated several times successfully, then, as I had the
chair up about half way it slipped out of my hands and

Gertrude's head came down on the floor. Pouting and whimpering, she started off toward the kitchen, massaging the back of her head.

Gertrude was great for paper dolls that she cut out of newspapers. The dolls had wonderful eyes that shut and open. The face was made by doubling the paper over, clipping the edge where the eyes were, and raising up the piece that formed the eyelids. When Gertrude wanted her dolls to go to sleep she pushed the eyelids down.

In Gertrude's cupboard in the kitchen, under the counter shelf, was kept her rag doll, William. He was about three feet high, had a gray face, painted eyes and a brown checkered suit. His hair, sewn to his head, had evidently been taken from an old stuffed cushion. Altogether he resembled a long, lanky colored boy.

Eugene ("Gene" for short), colored and eighteen, was supposed to be the gardener and take care of horses. He was always looking out for my welfare in every way.

Gene Duncan

Gene had a lot of half brothers and sisters, part Duncans and part Johnsons, and he was the flower of the Duncan family. He took good care of the horses, but there were just some things he could not do well. One was mowing the lawn. He always left streaks of uncut grass.

Gene was the quickest-moving piece of human flesh that I ever saw in my life. One day, on our way home from Poughkeepsie, he actually chased and caught four gray squirrels with a horsewhip as they were running on a rail fence. He was first on one side of the fence, then on the other.

Another time, one of us shot at a partridge and missed it, and it flew over Eugene's head. He jumped up and grabbed it and fell over a fence with it. Gene could jump farther than anyone I knew.

It was a job to keep him dressed neatly, as he would

wear torn shirts. He was tall and slender and squirmy as an eel, chuck full of laughter.

Out by the main road were some old locust stumps that we were gradually digging out. A neighbor came and blasted them with gunpowder and we broke them to pieces with iron wedges. One spring morning when Gene and I were working at them, he decided to have his "haar" cut, and I told him I would do it.

I went across the road and borrowed a pair of scissors from Mrs. Sink, and while Gene sat in the wheelbarrow I cut his wool as close as I could get it. He earnestly warned me not to let the wool I clipped off scatter out of the wheelbarrow because the birds would get it to use in their nest building. If that happened, according to a popular superstition, he would go crazy.

But after the job was finished I scratched up the wool and ran up the road with it, scattering it in all directions, which caused much pouting on Gene's part.

Ann Wing's "town"

Gene came to us from Ann Wing, a woman who owned a farm of 1,400 acres, which she inherited from her husband, Obed Wing. This farm was run like a Southern plantation. It seemed alive with colored people, who lived in small houses along the road.

I never heard how all these colored people came to this locality, but presumed it might have been through the Underground Railway during Civil War times. (Just above that area many Quakers had settled.)

The Wings also owned the little place called "Town," which was the Chestnut Ridge post office. The buildings included the large, rambling white house where the Wings lived, its numerous red barns and outbuildings. Across the road from the barns was a large virgin grove of white oak trees that abounded in red and gray squirrels. The west side of these woods merged into a swamp lined with white birches and alder.

This swamp belonged to Henry Swift, a retired Northern Army captain. Swift and my father were talking, and he said a person should have a hobby, something one could work at all one's life. My father commented that Mr. Swift certainly had it in that swamp, as they were always clearing the bogs and burning them. Eventually they made a lovely pasture of it.

Down through this swamp and through the alder grove wound a wide ditch full of clear, never-failing water which was well stocked with redfin fish and eels.

At the intersection of the roads stood the country store, typical of that section. The store was long, rather narrow, with a deep porch in front. It was painted brown and had tight, green blinds or shutters, all with iron bars across them, which could be fastened from the inside with a pin. The store had the usual counters on each side, and stocks of calico, buttons, flour and salt in the back room, mixed with plowshares, and always a big round cheese in a wire netting case to keep the flies off. There were large, deep boxes, fitted with castors, that could roll under the counters. These were filled with brown and white sugar.

The country store at the crossroads

There was a shelf piled with overalls and cheap jeans, never fitting, and always smelling of stale tobacco juice. Another had crockery of outlandish pattern. Under these shelves, standing on the floor, was the barrel of soda crackers, which became more stale and broken as you got nearer the bottom.

In the corner stood some long-handled shovels, spading forks and ax handles. In the back room were oat and rye cradles for cradling grain. They hung over a crossbeam, their blades painted red and green. Hanging on pegs were wooden hay rakes (for grain) and a few oxbows.

In the middle of the store, between the counters, was a tall, swell-bodied cast iron stove. It was red hot all winter and surrounded by a few rickety chairs for chronic sitters. The floor was of wide spruce boards

57

with worn knots protruding. In all directions around the stove was a layer of matted and plastered-down tobacco cuds. Much of the tobacco sold here never left the store. Anywhere within ten feet of the stove the counters were whittled and names were carved.

Behind the counter stood John Cline, somewhat resembling Uncle Sam. John wore high leather boots, his trousers tucked inside them, a homemade shirt of checkered brown gingham, suspenders and a vest. His manner was pleasing, and he was accommodating in every way.

John Cline

John only showed agitation when the customer failed to bring a container for kerosene and he would have to lend a new jug. This store did a large trade because it was the only one within several miles.

In an ell was a bar, with a bartender in charge. From all accounts, an immense amount of liquor was sold. It was said that in earlier days, on Saturday nights, a barrel of rum would be brought here from Poughkeepsie. The barrel was never taken off the wagon, but was turned on its side and a spigot inserted. The entire contents was sold, drink by drink.

Across the road from the store, a bit further to the west, was the blacksmith's shop, presided over by Abe Wolven. He was a small, dried-up, gray-haired man, but very wiry. The colored children from Ann Wing's place would tease him, calling him names.

Abe Wolven, blacksmith

Beside the shop was a rack for shoeing oxen—really a set of stocks—as all well-equipped blacksmith shops had in those days. In the rear of the shop was a tangled mass of old wheels and buggy tops, and enveloping all was a general smell of pigweed and burdock.

Beyond the Crossroads, and down the road toward Clove Hollow, stood the Methodist Church, a plain, rectangular building with gable roof and short, square steeple. It was white, with green shutters. My father, though not a preacher, used to hold services there sometimes, when there was no one else to do it.

To the south, down the road that led to the mountain, was the millpond, sawmill and cider mill. This is the setting from which the main supply of our colored help came. If we were short any tool or piece of equipment in corn- cutting or planting time, Gene and I would drive down, at breakneck speed, to Ann Wing's, his old stamping ground. But after we reached there it would take about two hours to do all the borrowing, for there might be a little side trip into Swift's Swamp with the fish hooks to catch a few redfins. Or Gene might want to trade accordions with Neal, his half brother. And this trading all had to be done unbeknownst to Ann Wing. It necessitated Neal going up to his attic room and lowering the article to be traded out of the window by a string, sometimes into Gene's big straw hat. It seemed to me every building around there had either a little brown jug sitting on a beam, or a flat bottle tucked away somewhere. Eventually, those jugs and bottles became the ruination of the whole community. Gene, fortunately, never became a drinking man.

Colored help from Wing's

We were occasionally helped out by young Charlie Johnson, blacker than coal. He was so black he was blue, shone like a bottle. He was about two years older than I, and ferocious in appearance, especially when he rolled his eyes.

Charlie Johnson

Charlie would brag about the boys he had laid on their backs and beaten to a pulp. He really was a great wrestler. He was short, with an immense foundation, so when he spread his feet apart he covered so much ground that it was impossible to throw him.

One day he swept out the carriage house and horse stables, made a rack for the brooms and shovels, then printed out a sign with blue chalk and nailed it up on the post in the carriage house. It read: "Whoever spats on the floor will get frowed out quick."

Boy-like, I tested his threat, of course, and had no ill effects from the result of it.

Joe Duncan was another half brother, exceedingly cheerful and like Gene, quick as a flash. Joe was about twelve years old, always barefoot in the summer. Like Charlie, he helped us at odd times, and would stay with Gene for weeks as a volunteer in haying or planting.

Joe and I once tried to go into the harness business. He would go off and collect the harnesses to mend from the different neighbors, and I would stay home and sew them. Joe would help mend, also, and he would return the mended harness, making all the collections, which we would divide.

"Colored Johnson" was Charlie Johnson's father. Like his son, he was immensely strong. He could pick up a barrel of cider by the chimes and put it in a wagon.

He did not work for us, but we used to hear about his biting ten-penny nails in two, and lifting a barrel of flour by his teeth. But it may all have been hearsay.

Down below Ann Wing's, further in the mountain at the intersection of Stearn's Road, on a little grass road that branched off from the main highway there lived an old ex-slave by the name of Jackie Duncan.

He was not related to the Duncan boys who worked for us. His wife and son, Amos, showed Indian blood. Jackie was black as could be, with bushy gray hair. He lived in a house with a low, gabled roof that was patched almost beyond recognition. It was a larger house than most of the colored people had, covered with weatherbeaten horizontal siding and honeysuckle and grapevines. The garden patch in front of the house was full of sweet corn, vegetables, sunflowers and gourds.

Their occupation consisted mostly of selling wild berries and making all kinds of splint baskets, which they sold to the farmers in the surrounding country-side. It was said of Jackie that he could make a water-tight basket.

Amos often came to our place with all sizes of baskets and usually succeeded in making some kind of sale, as we used a great many. He was short, with a very large head, high cheekbones, and bright black eyes which were constantly moving. He stuttered considerably.

Often, when Amos came he would put his hand in his bright blue jumper jacket and suddenly whip out a little "teensie weensie" basket and give it to me. This one was a miniature of a larger basket, possibly not over an inch square. If it was not a tiny basket Amos brought, it was one of the big sweet bough apples, one of the earliest in our section.

Amos and his splint baskets

At The Ridge there always had to be replenishment of bushel baskets for corn-husking and half-bushel baskets for apple-picking and a basket about six inches wide and fourteen inches long, which we painted red, for our mother's garden basket. In this basket were always a pair of gloves, a trowel, a ball of cord and papers, and papers of seed.

One other basket we always had to be sure of having was my mother's key basket. This was about six inches square and four deep, with a strong handle. As I remember, it had keys enough in it for the Bastille, including keys for the house, the cake closet (a long spidery-looking key which still causes pleasant recollections), a duplicate to all the barn keys, and the tenant house key.

This basket and my mother were rarely separated. She also carried her unanswered letters in it. The basket was painted black and was varnished, with a little yellow stripe under the rim to match the furniture in her bedroom.

At forty, Poor Amos still had an undeveloped mind. After he had delivered his baskets he would sit for hours on the kitchen porch until we gently asked him if he didn't think it was time for him to go home. He would finally stutter and answer that he did, and would depart.

Up through the grass-covered Stearns Road leading past the old red Stearns house that belonged to the wagon maker Clinton Stearns, was the beginning of the Albert Tompkins farm. This was the first cleared land passing through birch, chestnut and oak woods from Jackie Duncan's.

Albert Tompkins' mail was addressed "Squire Tompkins." He was justice of the peace and greatly respected.

Just before reaching his cleared land, the road was lined with hazelnut bushes. From there, the road became less grassy and later there was no grass at all.

On the Tompkins place lived an old ex-slave in a dirt cellar dug into the side of the hill. The cellar was covered over with logs, holding a sloping roof of earth. The door was of rough boards hung on heavy hinges.

A fomer slave

This old man never could tell his age, and I can't remember him ever uttering a word. He had lived there for years, perfectly faithful and contented, working there as long as anyone could remember. He wore high rubber boots the year round, even in the hottest haying time weather. He was large, well built and had bushy gray hair and whiskers.

This man lost his life in the line of duty, working his way from the house to the barn in the face of a driving snow storm in order to do the milking. He went out at five in the afternoon, and about two hours later was found on a neighbor's porch. He had evidently missed the barn, wandered across a field and had seen the neighbor's light. He had died for lack of strength to make his presence known.

Death in the snow

The roads were so blocked with snow that it was six days before his frozen body could be removed by ox teams through the heavy drifts.

Studies of childhood objects, from memory, by Thomas Lossing, showing the cat Tiger in the Boston rocker, and Billy, the rocking horse.

Chapter VI
PETS AT THE RIDGE

"Chuckie" was my pet woodchuck. He had been caught in a trap that was set for larger woodchucks, and he was so small that the trap shut over the top of his back and caught him by a pinch of gray fur and hide. He was then only the size of a meadow mole.

I fed him milk, which he readily learned to drink out of the lid of a baking powder can. He wouldn't allow the lid to be taken away until every drop was gone. He would protest by taking hold of the edge of the lid, then hang on and whistle.

Chuckie, my pet woodchuck

At first, Chuckie's nose was about the shape of a squirrel's, but became much larger after he was grown. His ears were small and close to his head, his body short and very fat, covered with gray-brown fur. His legs were short, and his tail was a little brush, which when he was frightened would fluff out like a cat's.

Chuckie only knew Edward Bradford and me. To us he was perfectly tame, and when he was small we used to carry him in our pockets where he would go to sleep. Then one had better not disturb him or he would bite and whistle right in the pocket.

When we fed him apples he sat up on his hind legs, put one paw on the stem of the apple and ate a row out all the way around, turning it all the while. In this way he would reach the seeds, which he thought were delicious. Then he threw the remainder away. He would sit up like that and take a long spear of clover and poke it in his mouth, chewing off the leaves as he came to them. He kept poking it in his mouth until he got to the last of it, then would suddenly pull out the stem intact, without a leaf on it.

If there was a stranger near while he was eating, Chuckie kept his eye on him, bushed his tail out and made a funny chattering noise. His eyes were bright and shiny, just like shoe buttons.

Chuckie's summer cage

Our woodchuck was kept in a tin-lined wooden box with a wire all across the front, the box fastened to the vegetable garden fence. He lived this way all summer, but when the cold weather came his cage was fastened up in the warm cow stable, where he showed great uneasiness. Maybe he missed his summer companion, the little cottontail rabbit that had shared his cage and later mysteriously disappeared.

In the stable, Chuckie kept gnawing and chewing his cage, working at the wires. Finally, he was missing. The winter months passed, springtime came and one morning, after milking, what did we spy but Chuckie drinking out of the cat dish just under the stable door! In an instant he was gone down a hole under a beam. For a few days in a row this happened right after milking, so Edward and I decided to watch by the hole with a bag and grab him.

Edward successfully did this, and with great whistling and chattering Chuckie at first bit him, then almost immediately recognized he was with his friends. So we put him back in his cage out on the garden fence, where he seemed contented. Sometime in June the buttercups came into full bloom and one morning we hurriedly pulled some, leaves and stems and all, and put them in his cage. We were never really sure what happened, but these seemed to poison him, and he went into a stupor for a day and died.

The first cat I remember was General Grant, a tortoise shell.

General Grant, the cat

One New Year's Eve we had General Carrington as a houseguest, and I embarrassed my father by coming to him in the presence of General Carrington and reporting that General Grant was dead. (This was before President Ulysses S. Grant died in 1885. Ed.) The next cat was Ulysses, large and yellow, a great warrior, who lived a number of years, though battle-torn. Over time, he developed a croupy sneeze. He slept on a small blue blanket under the window near the bookcase in the library. He eventually learned that if he sneezed too long and loudly on a cold winter's night we would put him outside, and he had to find a spot in the woodshed. Preferring to stay in the house, he thought it best to smother his cough, which he did by crossing both front paws over his mouth.

Finally, his fur began to come out and a general disability developed. We young ones never knew how or when he disappeared.

Tiger came next, the cat most vivid in my recollection. He was our house cat, but at the barn were twenty-three cats, all of them wild. Tiger often came back from the barn in a rather dilapidated condition from being chastised by these outdoor ruffians.

More cats

He stood by us for quite some time. He was long and, except for his light gray coat, looked much like a tiger.

Then we suddenly possessed Tennessee and Vandalia.

They were named after prominent ships in the navy at that time. Vandalia was snow white and rather lackadaisical, never accomplishing much of anything. Tennessee was a little tiger cat. I never before heard of a cat that was such a good ratter and mouser. She was well aware of her good rating, and consequently was thoroughly independent and growled if interfered with. But she was a warm friend of mine and we were always together.

Tennessee was invariably on hand early in the morning to go with me after the cows, sometimes through long wet grass in which she looked more like a drowned rat than a cat. The chilliness made her howl to be picked up, and then she would ride on my shoulder.

During warm summer months there was a frog pond we had to pass on the way up the lane. It was about two feet deep, twenty wide and fifty long, and was a wonderful joy to frogs and peepers. On this pond I sailed little craft of various descriptions, from small sloops to three-masted schooners, and one masterpiece — a canvas canoe about three feet long and ten inches wide, painted black. The canoe floated lightly, and it occurred to me one day that perhaps Tennessee would enjoy a ride in it across the pond.

Cat and canoe

So I placed her in the canoe, she registering no great objections. I gave the boat a shove out onto the pond, calculating I had pushed it hard enough to land her on the other side. But as soon as Tennessee left the shore the most unearthly wail went up, the canoe rocking from side to side. The cat took hold of the gunwales on each side with both paws, keeping equilibrium with her head as she neared the other side.

She tried to make the other shore by jumping, but kicked the little boat out from under her as she jumped and landed in the nice warm water. She soon did reach the shore. This was repeated every evening, at first under protest from Tennessee, but finally she seemed to enjoy it. She used to stand in the water and walk along the edge of the pond, catching grasshoppers.

Tennessee and her antics

One night I was feeding a lamb and had a little pitcher of milk for filling the lamb's bottle. While I wasn't looking Tennessee crowded her head into the pitcher. Unable to pull it out, she ran with it across the barn floor until I was able to relieve her of it.

Another time I walked up on the porch and opened the door of the kitchen, which was kept cool and dark, and there I saw Tennessee on the shelf of the cupboard with one front paw down in a quart pitcher of cream. When she saw me she laid her ears flat and began to growl, as much to say, "What in the world did you come round for?" She kept taking out her paw, licking it and growling until I finally scatted her off.

Poor Tennessee was hunting in some very heavy grass one day while I was mowing with a scythe and I accidentally cut her leg. She started on a run to the barn, but I caught her and was able to dress her leg. By using much good sense in leaving the bandages alone, she recovered perfectly.

One descendant of Tennessee was named Little Gray, a cute ball of fur, with little blue eyes. She would explode if you touched her, but she was like her mother and always followed me.

Castor
and
Pollux

Castor and Pollux (Polly for short) were other cats, supposedly of a very good breed, imported from the adjoining town. It was thought worthy to exhibit them at the Dutchess County fair. Castor was a slim tiger cat, and Polly was yellow and stout.

Io, our full-blooded Jersey cow, was also taken to the county fair, a distance of eight miles. The weather was fine and the two cats were put in a large, square bird cage and placed on the hind end of the buckboard, near where Io was tied.

J.C., a hired man of grouchy disposition, was assigned to deliver this livestock to the officers of the fair. When J.C. arrived there, Io was placed in the cow shed with plenty of straw and behind a good manger, and the cats were put on exhibition in their cage, standing on a long table in the agricultural hall. The rest of this table was loaded with pumpkins, squash, large beets and onions and some cases of strained honey and a clear mess of pickles.

J.C. was boarded nearby for the four days of the fair. In the middle of the third day, when the east wind was blowing and the scuds were drifting northward, torrents of rain began to fall. The fairgrounds turned into mud ponds, the race course was abandoned, and the next afternoon saw none of us but J.C. at the fair. We stayed at home waiting for the return of our animals in the cold, drenching rainstorm.

J.C. gets
soaked
at the
fair

About four o'clock we saw from our library window the buckboard with the cage behind and its two small wet figures, like drowned rats. The halter was dragging in the mud, and there was no Io. I rushed out of the kitchen door and ran down the road just as J.C. was slamming the bird cage with the cats down on the ground and saying between his teeth, "Last time I'll ever take stuff to the fair!"

His long overcoat was soaked through, and his neck seemed longer than ever, his moustache more be-

70

draggled. The rain was coming down in sheets, and poor J.C. drove off to the barn with the horse. He was faced with the prospect of walking back, nobody knew how far, in search of the wandering Io.

I picked up the yowling cats and brought them into the kitchen, letting the forlorn creatures loose on the floor near the warm stove. They began to lick their coats and meditate. Meanwhile Io walked into the yard, bellowing, and was soon yanked into the barn by J.C., who was never again called upon to exhibit our animals at the fair.

Ole Bull was our canary, a very good singer, and he gave credit to his name. His cage hung on a bracket in the dining room all winter and came out on the front porch in the summer.

Ole Bull, the canary, and birds

He survived cat attacks on his cage. I especially remember one cat landing on the cage; the bottom dropped out, falling with the cat in a bedlam of bird seed and water, cuttlefish and chickweed. Ole Bull knew enough to stay in the top of the cage.

He lived to be twelve or thirteen years old before he weakened and died.

Ritter was our next canary, named after Professor Ritter in the music department at Vassar College. Like Ole Bull, he was worthy of his name.

Ritter also went through a cat cyclone, but not as successfully as Ole Bull, for he broke his leg. My sister made two fine splints from matches and bound them with white thread. Ritter entirely recovered and we had him for four or five years.

One day during a strong wind we were startled when a partridge flew from cedar trees in a corner of the yard straight through a dining room window pane and hit my mother on the shoulder.

We kept this bird in a cage for a few days, but he seemed so forlorn that we soon let him go.

Another time during a heavy rain and wind storm I found a dead partridge on the east side of the house, where he had apparently struck the wall.

Peter, the little Berkshire pig, was very gentle. He was one of ten descendants of the sow Judy, and like her was nearly all black.

Peter had a great sense of self-preservation and was a leader, taking his followers from one apple tree to another, making paths through the grass. When surprised, they all would go "Snort! Snort!" and run off as fast as their legs could carry them, then—like all little pigs when they think someone is after them—would suddenly turn and zig-zag in another direction.

Peter, the pig who milked cows

One evening Edward was milking Leone out in the barnyard when Peter, then about sixteen inches long, looked up wistfully at him. So Edward squirted milk on Peter's nose, and the pig opened his mouth and came closer, drinking it in with his eyes shut, as much to say "How delicious!"

This was the beginning. The very next milking found a contentedly grunting Peter traveling along toward the cow and Edward, to be rewarded by having milk again squirted at his nose. This kept up for several days, and Peter got so well acquainted and was such an attractive, clean little thing that I trained him to sit on an upturned bucket—for which he was rewarded with grains of corn. He needed little training, however, for he was too smart all by himself.

Later, Edward reported that Leone seemed to be dry mornings, yet had plenty of milk at night when she was brought from pasture. This mystified everyone and for days no one was able to explain it. One morning I went out to the barnyard early and found Leone and other cows still lying down, and Mr. Peter was also lying down, helping himself to a drink of milk from the non-objecting Leone!

Dickie the ram and his flock of sixteen sheep were so tame that we couldn't do anything with them.

We let them run in the cow stable at night, and if you put hay on your fork and started to fodder the cattle, the sheep would crowd around and pull it all off. They liked to pick out all the clover.

One day the whole flock went from the small barn toward the lane, all except one lamb, who ran around the corner of the barn, thinking the flock was following. Then he ran back to the barn again, and we had to drive him out. Again and again the lamb persistently went the wrong way, thinking it was where the flock had gone. Then he came back to the barn. We finally had to shut the door, catch him and carry him down the lane and show him his flock, he blatting the whole time from fright and loneliness. When he saw the flock, his tune changed to one of contentment.

In March of 1888, during the worst snowstorm ever known in our vicinity, a lone rooster was hatched under the deep foliage of spruce trees. We named him Blizzard. He grew to be lank and homely, white with brown wings, his green eyes resembling keyholes, a determined expression to his bill.

Blizzard was part Shanghai, a tall breed, and he was able to stand on the ground and eat off a flour barrel. He was a tame and familiar sight for years. I had very little interest in chickens, for every hen that I ever set with eggs came off three days before they should have and went around clucking as if the brood were following. Meanwhile the eggs were cooling in the nest.

Hawkeye was our first dog, arriving in the world the same day I did, and we were companions for fourteen years. He was considered a shepherd dog, had brown eyes, was black and tan with smooth lop ears and an Eskimo dog's tail.

Hawkeye had no particular accomplishment except to drive cattle, fight other dogs, and sit on a snowbank and bay at the moon all night. He never hunted, except for meadow moles, and never did catch a woodchuck. He was possessed to lie on the landing of the stairs at the risk of our lives, for we all stepped on him. Then he would jump and howl and lie down on the landing again. Whether outside or in, Hawkeye seemed to stay on the side of the house where he could best guard us children and Mother.

Hawkeye was deathly afraid of Fourth of July noises or thunder. On one occasion I found him hidden in the ash pan in the range, an old cookstove that was only used on state occasions. He liked ginger snaps better than anything else and would do anything for one. He would play hide-and-seek with the children if he could be rewarded with a ginger snap.

Finally, when he was fourteen years of age, I found him wandering in a swamp about two miles from the house. There I gave him his last meal of ginger snaps and he died.

Some of our family dogs

Bessie was a collie, given to us by a friend who was going to Europe. It was not long before she was taken with distemper, which caused her death. She and Mother were greatly attached to each other. If I would look at Bessie, she would go over and put a paw on Mother's knee.

Argus was purchased to take the place of Hawkeye. He was jet black and of no particular breed, with yellow eyes that looked like screwheads. He would chase everything he saw and delighted in chewing my cousin's legs. He finally developed fits, and that ended him in a couple of months time.

Then came Mauwee, a full-blooded Gordon setter, whose mother had taken first prize at the Brooklyn Dog Show. The name Mauwee was an Indian name for partridge.

Mauwee was given to me by my brother-in-law when she was a puppy, so small that when she was handed down from the wagon I could hold her right in my two hands. At the same time, my brother-in-law gave me a book with training rules. I immediately took it into the house, the little dog waddling after me, and placed the book on a table in the parlor.

Mauwee and her hunting

That first afternoon we were all playing tennis, and who should come toddling across the lawn with her head up and the instruction book in her mouth, but Mauwee, headed straight for me, as much as to say, "Please start training me."

Mauwee was exceedingly bright. According to the book, I was to start training her at the end of three months, and then for only fifteen minutes a day. Mauwee learned very rapidly, and soon knew all the rules of hunting and obeyed them perfectly. She grew to be black and tan, with lovely lines.

I never hunted with her myself, but my brother-in-law and others did, and she was excellent. In time, she was observed by a lieutenant in the navy, who often came to our house and owned a Laverick setter pup. He asked if I would train his dog, named Bina. This I did and found it no trouble at all, as he followed Mauwee's example.

This setter was with us about a year, but was poisoned by strychnine a neighbor had spread across a field to kill crows.

Aside from hunting, Mauwee learned all kinds of tricks, and she was a good dog to drive cows. Against my mother's wishes, she stayed in my room at night. One cold night she was left in the dining room, and when I came down in the morning I discovered our turkey-red tablecloth was missing from the table. I saw a bundle on the floor by my mother's chair with two squinty brown eyes looking up at me and hoping I would say nothing—and I couldn't.

Mauwee was a good woodchuck dog, but she would drink milk from the same wooden bowl with Chuckie, my tame woodchuck. Mauwee used to go upstairs to get my slippers for me, sometimes going so fast she would miss a step and tumble. She even learned to preach: I would put a book on top of a high stepladder and she would climb up, put her paws on the book and howl. Mauwee was taught with the reward of oyster crackers. When I told her to get down, she usually jumped from the top of the ladder, kicking it over, rushing around the room and scattering the rugs in delight.

Training dogs to hunt, preach and drive

Mauwee went driving with me in an open box wagon, she sitting alongside me on the seat, holding the lines in her teeth. The horse was gentle, listening to me talk to Mauwee about birds, woodchucks, rats and squirrels. Our conversation was exciting at time, and as I would emphasize squirrels or woodchucks she would watch my face, give a little squeal and shudder of excitement.

I would be talking along to her, fooling about something, and she would actually grin on one side of her face. One day while she was holding the lines, Mauwee spied a squirrel on the fence, and without warning jumped out with the lines and started chasing the squirrel.

I trained Mauwee and Bina, the Laverick setter, to be harnessed to a small two-wheeled cart. For some reason, Mauwee always thought this beneath her dignity. Bina would sit in the cart on his hind legs and drive Mauwee on a dog-trot up the road, with garden twine for lines. The motion made Bina's head bob, yet he would maintain the grandest air in the world.

I used to hunt eggs in the barn, put them in a basket, and let Mauwee carry it to my sister in the house. Mauwee would walk carefully, wagging her tail all the way.

Our neighbors, the Russels, had a big old goat named Billy that they used to run the treadmill of the swing churn. Every few days they unchained Billy from the long wire where he was tethered and put him on the treadmill. This was a horizontal wooden disk, tilted on a slope, the weight of Billy making it turn as it was geared to the churn. He was hitched to a stationary crossbar and had to keep walking slowly as the wheel went out from under him.

Borrowing Billy the goat

Billy was very independent. If we hitched him to a cart and he happened to see a piece of clover that he wanted, he would go after it and take us with him. There was a certain patch of white clover that he just loved to eat, and he would go there in spite of all our strength trying to hold him back. We had a cart with four iron wheels, which made it hard to pull, but that did not stop Billy when he made up his mind to go someplace. I was always borrowing him when he was not needed for churning.

One day the chain I was trying to lead him by got wrapped around my hand, with my thumb through the ring, and he dragged me across the lawn to his patch of clover before he stopped. Another time, he got me fast with the chain around my waist, and he kept pulling to get fresh grass that was out of his reach, squeezing me unmercifully.

I was afraid of Billy, afraid he would run away with me, but I was forever borrowing him and he was forever abusing me.

"Sleigh Riding on the Hudson," by Benson Lossing.

Chapter VII
HORSES AND CATTLE

When I was about eleven, we had a black Jersey cow, Isis, who lost her cud until my nurse, Mrs. Mott, from Brooklyn, gave her a cloth bag of grass to chew on. That brought back the cud. Isis was always anemic, and gave only about a quart of milk. Still, we kept her about ten years.

Cows and bull calves

Leone was another cow, partly Guernsey, and the cosiest little cow that ever lived. She was a sweet-looking little thing, and had horns like a bug, so we called her "Bughorn." Blair, her calf was even cosier than she, and was nicknamed "Cosy."

Angelique was a sister of Isis, rather slim and very strong. She would kick every time you looked at her, but she gave an immense amount of milk. When

Angelique was a calf the door of her pen blew open one sub-zero night, and her ears and tail froze. Eventually, half those ears and half the tail dropped, but she was Angelique, just the same.

We bought Old Pine when she was about fifteen. She was old enough to vote and had countless rings on her horns. Old Pine was a registered Jersey, and when we paid twenty dollars for her we thought we got a bargain. She would walk right through a fence anywhere, a regular battering ram, and she hollered all the time for her calf, though she dried up within three weeks after having one.

After she had a calf, Old Pine was always delirious for weeks. Her eyes were glassy and we couldn't wean the calf because she would break in and get her away. As a consequence we always let her have the calves and turned them both out by the woods.

Old Pine certainly did have some nice calves, and they acted as though they were of royal blood. They were swank and showed their breeding. One of her calves was named Breakfast because when she got old enough we used to milk her first for breakfast.

One of the bull calves got wild, just like a real wild animal. I found him one day lying on his side, sound asleep, his legs twitching. I got down on my knees and was talking to him and he began to move, gradually opening his eyes. When he realized it was I he jumped up and ran away as fast as he could.

Taming a bull calf

I decided to tame him and brought him up to the barn with all the cattle and Old Pine, his mama. I left the barn door open, knowing the snoopy disposition of his mama. Both soon walked inside and I watched until mama came out. Then I slammed the door. The calf was on the big thrashing floor, a great open space that formed the arena, and the bullfight was on. I was going to walk in and lasso him.

The spectators were thirteen-year-old Edward and my

cousin, Warner Titus, eight years old. They were sitting on a beam to watch the roping. But instead of my roping the calf, he chased me, and over the beam I went, into the hay mow, making a hairsbreadth escape. Meanwhile, Warner slipped down and ran out a side door, hollering for help.

Within three or four days, I had that animal so he would come up to me and take an ear of corn out of my hand. I didn't give him anything to eat except out of my hand. He would call until he couldn't call anymore, until his voice was gone. I set a little water in a pail, not much, just inside the door. When he came and drank it, I handed him some corn, more and more at a time. This was done with the door open a crack.

Finally, I could sit in the door with it wide open and he would come up and eat all he wanted. Then he would come to me any time I called him, and we got to be great friends. I think I eventually sold him for an ox team.

Starlight and Moonlight were steers we raised from little calves. Starlight was marked the clearest I have ever seen in any animal. Supposed to be Holstein, he was chestnut and white. They were about the same size, but Moonlight was not so pretty, a kind of reddish gray.

Starlight and Moonlight and Dickie the ram

Dickie the ram hated Starlight. When Dickie saw Starlight across a field, he would stampede for him and throw his head up to hit him. Dickie invariably missed because Starlight was a little too high for his horns. That would throw Dickie over backward and cause him to kick Starlight with his hind feet. Starlight never paid any attention, and Dickie would fall on his back every time.

Edward was the first to train Starlight and Moonlight as an ox team. He put a little yoke on them when they were calves. We had a two-wheel cart, and every night Edward would go out in it to visit his traps. That was some outfit—the cart with handsome Starlight and Moonlight and good-looking little Edward, black as a blackberry, sitting up in the cart in his blue jumper.

There was just a board between the two wheels for Edward to sit on. He drove a half-mile radius to visit his woodchuck traps, across the green meadows, returning about sundown with a few woodchucks hanging on the axle.

The oxen Damon and Pythias

Damon and Pythias were a big team of red oxen, weighing 3,600 pounds when they were thin and in good working condition. Damon never let Pythias get a step ahead of him and kept looking at him all the time.

That team really seemed proud of what they could pull. Damon measured two feet four between his horns. He was lying down one day and Edward sat down on his head and took hold of each horn. Just then the ox decided to knock a fly off his back and threw little Edward about ten feet.

One day I found Pythias had in some way caught his horn in the ground. He had turned halfway over on his back, impaled there. I had to pull his horn out of the ground and help him get away.

Egypt and Memmon

Another pair of oxen were named Egypt and Memnon.

Egypt was black, with horns going straight up, resembling a devil, which he was. Memnon was yellow. They could jump any fence, even together with the yoke on. Egypt would get out of any place you put him. I found him in the garden one day, so I put him in the stable in the stanchion, fastened with a block of wood dropping back of the bar. Then I hid and quietly watched him.

He listened for a while to make sure no one was there, then raised his straight horn beside the bar of the stanchion and pushed it up, pushing the bar out. He backed out, and with his horn unhooked the door, went out to the barnyard, jumped over the gate and walked to the garden.

When Egypt got tired plowing he would lie down and rest, then would get up and go on again. When Egypt slept in the furrow, Memnon would stand with his head tipped in the yoke to accommodate him. The result was that Egypt was always fat and Memnon was always thin. How oxen will figure how to get something to eat and will scheme for their own welfare!

We used to say that cattle were like human beings, all classes, from the aristocracy down to the most meek and apologetic when trying to get something to eat.

This pair got so troublesome that I traded them to Neddie Butler for a Montana horse. I drove them down the eight miles, reaching Butler's before night, then drove the horse home. The next morning was foggy, and as I walked out to the barn in the early hours I saw a dark spot under an apple tree. Lo and behold Egypt had returned! He was calmly chewing his cud, with both horns sticking straight up. I sent word to Butler, and in a few days he came after him.

Fannie and Katie were two of our horses, both jet black.

Our horses Fannie and Katie

Fannie was named after my aunt, but was of an entirely different disposition. My aunt was very sweet and mild, but Fannie was "a damned old vixen," according to what Jesse Vridenburg said when she ran off in the fog as he was trying to hitch her to the carriage to take my father to the train. She ran away that day and rolled in a semi-dry frog pond, harness and all. Katie, missing her mate, went in another direction to look for her.

Their original driver was Morris, colored, who came with them when we bought them from my uncle. While Morris was buckling the neck yoke strap one morning, Fannie picked Morris up by the hair of his head.

It seemed that team ran away every chance they got, but they never ran away with my father. They were afraid of everything, would turn around if they could when they saw a railroad train. But my father would drive them with his eyes shut, taking the opportunity to rest his eyes. He always drove with a nagging motion of the reins, and Fannie would counteract it by always nagging the other way.

Once, Fannie was frightened by a barrel standing beside a bridge, so my father took my little sister out of the buggy and stood her in the corner of the fence until he could persuade Fannie to pass the barrel. Then he went back and got my sister and put her in the buggy again.

My first time driving a sleigh

Having never before harnessed a horse, I decided one day—when nobody was around—to harness Katie to the sleigh and take Helen for a ride. I did it and drove up to the front door for her to get in.

We set off, and Katie seemed particularly gay, at first traveling in little spurts, then slowing to her usual gait. We drove down to Phelp's Line, a perfectly straight road for half a mile. Then we turned around and started back again, Katie gaining speed all the time. Soon I heard a bump and a bump, and Katie's tail was switching.

Then she began to run, and I realized the sleigh was harnessed too close to her heels, and they were striking. The faster she ran the harder her heels struck. Soon, we were nearing the barn, the doors being parallel to the road. I endeavored to steer Katie into the door, cat-a-corner, the sleigh striking the doorpost, throwing the horse in and us out. I never measured how far. At any rate, it was a happy ending to the agony we had gone through.

When I was ten years old, my sister and I were driving with Fannie down to Dover, with the snow all gone except for a small patch in a hollow by the roadside. Fannie spied it and immediately backed off the bank.

This threw everything off the wagon and threw the seats out, sister going up like a rocket and down on her head into a patch of blackberry bushes.

A broken arm, lucky escape

Next I knew the hub of the wagon was on my shoulder and Fannie's heels were stamping around my head and also stamping around a roll of Father's valuable drawings, which my sister was taking to exhibit at the Academy of Design in New York.

By instinct I grabbed the package, pulled my head back, and got out from under the wagon to unharness the horse. But my arm was broken and dislocated at the shoulder.

Eventually, Katie passed away from her many spasms of colic, and Fannie was pensioned at the age of thirty-three. We bought Mohegan, a chestnut and very strong at eight years old. We bought him from a dealer to be the mate of Bonnie, who had been purchased three years before and proved to be a jewel of a horse in every way.

Bonnie was a model bay horse, a good traveler, always intent upon his own business and full of good horse sense. Once he got caught on a barbed wire fence and I found him the next morning, wide-eyed but standing perfectly still, willing to wait while I cut the wire.

Bonnie's nemesis was a blue Montana horse that was marked like a zebra. Montana would jump right on Bonnie and bite him, would even tear Bonnie's blanket off. Montana did this once when he caught Bonnie drinking out of his trough, rushing across the barnyard to do it.

The horse Montana

Montana was a large black horse that we got from a dealer who got him from Montana. He was contented to paw through the snow and eat old dead grass instead of sweet hay. He ran outdoors all winter. Once he had a canopy of snow about six inches thick on his back, and icicles hanging along the edges, where the heat of his body had melted the snow. His coat was very heavy. When I felt sorry for him and gave him a bunch of nice, sweet hay, he immediately turned his back on me and it, walked off and pawed down through the snow to eat the frozen grass.

That spring he was broken in for plowing.

Mohegan, the chestnut, had splendid qualities. He was strong, with great endurance, and was kind, but he lacked speed. Bonnie always kept about four inches in front of him. Mohegan tried, and really went further than Bonnie as far as up-and-down motion is concerned. If he thought you were going to touch him with the whip he would lay his ears back, adding to the up-and-down motion.

Mohegan, a splendid chestnut horse

One day our dog Mauwee bit the mailboy, and we thought it best to take the boy at once to the doctor to have the wound tended. My brother harnessed Mohegan to a phaeton and a hurried three-mile trip to the doctor began. There was a long hill to go down, and as they started down it the breeching broke and Mohegan at once started running.

My brother began pulling her off the side of the road, saw a big rock ahead, so pulled her into the road again just in time, but a front wheel hit the rock. This threw my brother out with the reins, and away went Mohegan, the helpless mailboy riding along, without any positive destination in view. The phaeton went out of sight around a bend, my brother following on the run.

Around that bend he found the phaeton against a rock and right side up, but with no wheels. The mailboy was sitting dazed in the seat with the leather dashboard turned over on his knees. The horse was at the foot of the hill, quietly grazing on spring grass.

Montana got Bronco as a mate, purchased from a

farmer who told me of his shortcomings before I bought him. Afterwards I realized his warnings were true.

Bronco

Bronco was about eight years old when he came into our possession. He had given up his free life on the western plains and accepted the more prosaic routine of the farm, plowing, mowing, and cultivating crops all through the spring and summer. He was not very large, a light slate blue in color, and had a dark brown crosslike pattern on his back. His eyes were large, with a gentle expression. He had a heavy neck in proportion to his size, and when he took the bit in his teeth it was almost impossible to hold him.

I can think of no fault he had other than to run away. My sisters would groom him and begged me to let them drive him, but I had misgivings about his inner spirit. I repeatedly refused to let my sisters drive "dear Bronco," until their pleadings so pestered me that I said yes.

For some weeks their enjoyment was great as they drove over the hills, gazing at the landscape and the beautiful flowers. One fine autumn afternoon, my sisters drove through a village, Bronco jogging along and seeming almost asleep, my sister later said. He must have been dreaming of life on the plains, for he suddenly bucked and started, both sisters' heels flying up, Bronco on a run. Fortunately they steered him under a store shed where the timely help of a gentleman prevented him from running over other horses and wagons hitched there.

My one sister being a natural-born Jehu, and the other disturbed at nothing, probably explains why they soon started out again on the open road with Bronco. He traveled as docilely as one might wish for half a mile, then had another dream and my sister had to beach him by running head on to a sandbank.

Both sisters were thrown out, one landing on the gravel, the other on the crossbar of the shafts, the robe wrapped tightly around her feet. Bronco was plunging

Another crash

87

as she tried to untangle, and by the time she could step on terra firma the horse was gone, the wagon deposited upside down off a small bridge. Some distance beyond they found the shafts and harness, Bronco quietly grazing beside the road.

During the remainder of that fall and winter, Bronco was never groomed.

Lightning strikes our horses

In spring, Bronco and Montana were used as a team for plowing, working diligently and well. All through haying their work was satisfactory. Then, in a heavy electric storm one night near the last of August, I heard Bronco whinnying. At daylight I went through the wet grass to see what had happened. Along the lane where the horses were pasturing several fence posts were shattered to pieces, thirty-six in all marred by lightning.

Bronco was in the lane, but Montana was gone, the fence wires being down. By following his tracks I found him standing in a bunch of elderberry bushes. When I led him out all four legs were very stiff, and he stood very much like a saw horse. From then on we turned him out in a pasture by the woods, where he steadily improved until I sold him back to his original owner.

Later, almost entirely recovered, Montana was used to draw heavy loads of stone for the construction of a hotel.

Ticklish Peggy

Peggy was a thin little black horse, about seven years old, with bright eyes. Her ears were small and covered with fuzz, like a mouse.

Peggy was thin-skinned and terribly ticklish, so no blacksmith could shoe her without tying her up. To them she had the reputation of being "an ugly brute." In reality, she was of a very sweet disposition, but so ticklish that she buffaloed almost everyone.

Her former owner managed to be sober once in a while. He was found one morning lying over the shafts of his wagon, Peggy quietly grazing, waiting for him to sober up enough to drive on. This incident, among others, made me decide there was nothing really ugly about Peggy, which later was proven to be right.

My sisters drove Peggy in all sorts of places, and she was an excellent traveler. At one point this was recognized by a doctor who offered me a hundred and fifty dollars for her.

Peggy did have one admissible defect: She could not see well in the dark. The consequence was that when my sister and the colored girl, Hattie, were driving home one night with the groceries, Peggy went too near to the edge of the bridge, so all three landed in the brook—my sister and Hattie in the top of the buggy and Peggy on her side. Peggy knew enough to lie still until a neighbor helped them out. They went on without a scratch.

One day, we children had a parade on the farm. We were able to muster six pair of cattle, ranging in size from yearling calves to Damon and Pythias, our large old pair.

A parade of children and farm animals

They were all pulling some kind of cart as we paraded from the barn up to the house, passing in front of the horse block, which was the old stone mantle from my great-grandmother's fireplace. On this day it served as the reviewing stand.

My two sisters were the judges and the occupants of the reviewing stand. My brother, Edward and I were the drivers of the six pair of cattle, which were kept in line with a long rope running through the rings of all the yokes. Another time I drove up to this stone mantle with a calf hitched to a two-wheeled cart made of wagon wheels, with a square body. This calf was Io, then aged one year.

I asked Helen to get in and take a ride. She accepted the invitation, but as we started off one of the garden twine lines broke, and instead of the calf following the driveway, she began to blat and run down across the lawn and against a spruce tree, which turned the cart over.

I freed the frightened calf from the cart, and she ran out to the road and down the hill, out of sight.

"Mouth of Wappingi's Creek,"
by Benson Lossing

Chapter VIII
TRAPS, HUT AND BLIZZARD

One spring, before it was time to plow and plant, Edward and I set several traps for skunks. As there were over three hundred and forty acres in the farm, we would get up on the mill with a spyglass to examine our traps.

*Trapping
skunks
with
Edward*

If the one with the glass saw a dark object flopping in any of our traps, he would sing out to the one on the ground: "A skunk! A skunk!" The answer would be, "A club! A club!"

While one of us was scurrying after clubs the other would be sliding down the windmill. A breathless chase followed, across the brown fields in the direction of the object.

On one of these expeditions near a haystack, we found our pet cat, Tennessee, flopping a trap. As fortune would have it, she had caught most of her body in the trap and consequently was not hurt.

The upshot of our trapping was that we acquired many skunks, which of course had to be skinned. Owing to the excitement of being hunters of wild game, we overlooked the odors. We also lessened them by burning a pan of old rags while we worked.

Lingering, however, in the folds of our clothing and in our hair was something that painfully reminded our family of skunks. Our dogs Bina and Mauwee were never without the smell, especially on damp mornings. This smell must have been what made my sisters form a committee that waited on my mother and required the abolition of skunk trapping. At any rate, the committee demanded in no uncertain terms that skunk-trapping cease.

With the pelts to sell them

By this time we had a neat little boxful of pelts and a journey was planned to go to Poughkeepsie with them, as well as with some cow hides and with some tallow for the soap factory. Owing to the well-seasoned nose of the hide man we were not reprimanded while he examined the pelts. He shook his head so as to shake down the price. Most of these pelts were from "pitchfork skunks," he said, and therefore he had to make the price low, offering us fifteen cents a pelt. But two black ones brought us seventy-five cents each.

Edward and I were, of course, proud of our sale and although conscious of smelling something of skunk, we promptly treated ourselves to dinner at Smith's Restaurant, where we had fried oysters and other good things. To be sure he got his money's worth, Edward ate up all the pickles in the dish.

Then came the long, tedious drive home through the cold twenty miles, arriving home long after dark.

Edward and I once built a hut a half mile from the house, over in the woods. We first dug a hole in a good dry spot, then placed small logs around it in log cabin style, high enough to clear our heads.

Building a hut in the woods

Then we covered the whole roof with split shakes, and covered these with oak and chestnut leaves and earth on top of them, making a very warm cabin. Only three by seven feet, this cabin was to be used to eat our lunches when chopping firewood. At one end we had a milk can for a stove and a tin leader pipe for a stove pipe.

The stove was either red hot or cold, and the part that was soldered soon melted. In some unexplained manner, the stove stood up just the same.

For a seat we had two wide, split sticks across the cabin, in front of the fire, and had a supply shelf in the corner. For a door we had an old gray horse blanket. There was no window.

One January day when we were chopping wood in the sunshine near the cabin, we decided that after the next light snow we would come over and spend the night and go rabbit hunting early in the morning, when the tracks were fresh. Accordingly, in a few days the light snow began to fall. We provisioned ourselves with ham, coffee, condensed milk, bread, sugar, and some of Alvira's famous ginger snaps. We struck out for the woods, taking a blanket to reinforce the door.

With us was Mauwee and Bina and a shotgun—a muzzle-loader of my grandfather's. We got to the cabin just before dark, in the spitting snow. We searched for old dry stumps to split firewood from, storing it under our seat. We thought we had a great supply.

We arranged a round stick across the cabin for a back that we could lean against and imagined we would be entirely comfortable for the night. We retired until morning, expecting to hunt through the early hours.

During the night, about six inches of snow fell, heavily

*Snowmelt,
a stove
and burned
boots*

covering the roof. It became so warm inside that we had our coats off. Presently, we began to feel water dripping on us. The heat of the stove had melted the snow on the roof and it was running through the clay and leaves. This caused us to get back into our coats to keep from getting damp.

Thus we spent the early night hours. We talked over hunting, chopping wood, and what a wonderful trip we had had not so long ago on that twenty miles to Poughkeepsie with our load of hides and skunk skins. With part of the proceeds, I had purchased a pair of hightop leather boots, such as I had seen that day on some of the men working on the first bridge to cross the Hudson. Those boots cost five dollars and were fur-lined about the feet. They made me feel very tall that night in the cabin.

Pretty soon, we began to doze and leaned back for the night against our round stick. I have no idea what time it was, but far into the night we woke up in a mess of yells and squeals to find that the back of our seat had given way and we had fallen over backwards on Mauwee and Bina. In all that scrambling there was that gun mixed in with us. Our stove had gone out long ago, and the cabin was dark of course. We lit our lantern, shivering as we did so.

The light shone across the ceiling and we found that where water had been dripping there were now icicles hanging. We attempted to start a fire, but had no wood left. At this, Edward began to cry and wanted to go home and climb into the hay mow. But I wouldn't agree to it, as I would hate to meet my mother and sister under those circumstances.

So we threw back our horse blanket and emerged with our axes into the open. The night was bright with the snow on the ground, and it was still snowing. We again hunted out dry stumps and split off wood enough to keep us until morning. As soon as we got our fire going we were comfortable enough. We had a very early breakfast and enjoyed our hot coffee. With the dogs we went out to hunt rabbits, but found none. Upon reaching home we were informed we smelled like smoked ham. Then I noticed that my shins had evidently been too close to the stove while I was asleep, for my beautiful boots were spoiled, drawn out to a point and burned to a crisp.

Saturday, March the 10th, 1888, was a beautiful spring day with little if any snow in sight, except in the woods in the shady ravines.

The day before the blizzard

Edward and I were making bar posts out south of the house by the woodpile. We were talking as though spring had come for good, saying there would be no more snow and that frost was about out of the ground and we could soon begin plowing. The day was so pleasant my mother and sister drove about fifteen miles down to Leather Hill, which was a foothill of Quaker Hill, to visit Mary Titus, our cousin. They planned to return the following day.

Sunday, the 11th, was still warm, with drifting clouds and some blue sky, though there was an occasional squall of large, wet flakes of snow. This spitting snow and my cousin's invitation for them to remain until Monday caused my mother and sister to defer their start for home another day.

At home the barns were nearly empty of hay, except for one large mow of choice timothy which we had already sold to the Thornedale Stock Farm. We planned to start on Monday to fill from the stacks in the south meadow. As it got along toward night and my mother and sister had not arrived, we decided they had been very wise to wait until the snow squalls were over before they started home.

We awoke on Monday morning hearing the sound of driving snow against the window pane and it seemed as though it would never come daylight. We arose at the usual time and it was still dark and snowing hard. It was impossible to see through the snow that stuck to the windowpane, so we took our time in eating breakfast instead of following the usual custom of going to the barn first.

Even by the time we had finished breakfast, however, full daylight had not yet come. When Edwin, Edward and I left for the barn, a howling northwest wind was blowing and a wet snow was sticking to everything in sheltered spots, but from the spruce trees to the barn a bleak stretch of path was blown entirely free of snow. The barn, old wagon house and corn house were completely coated with snow sticking to the siding.

A howling northwest wind

Upon entering the barn we found the horses comfortable and warm. From there across the sheltered barnyard to the cow stable we had no difficulty in walking, there being only about six inches of snow on the level ground. We found the cattle contented and gave them a good feeding of hay. Then we realized that we must in some way get a load of hay from the stacks that morning as there was not enough for another feeding without breaking into that mow which had already been sold.

On the south and east sides of the barnyard was a high, tight, board fence, and the west and north sides were sheltered by the barn and stables. On the south side a gate opened into a two-acre lot, and just over the fence from this lot was the big south field with a stack of hay standing near the fence. The barn sheltered this little field for about half the distance to the stack, leaving the path swept by the wind and entirely free of snow.

Feeding stock in the storm

We yoked our oxen to a large sled, not knowing how we would manage a forkful of hay in all that wind. Then we drove around on the lee side of the stack and, by raising the hay into the wind, we could get under it. Finally, we got a load large enough to haul to the barn.

Meanwhile the weather had changed to an intense cold and the snow was fine, almost a hail. In spite of it we drew three or four loads of the hay, an amount we congratulated ourselves would take us over the storm.

It was now nearing noon and was darker than I had ever seen it at that time of day. The wind was howling through the locust and spruce trees and the fine snow was almost horizontal. The thermometer registered seven degrees above zero. By the middle of the afternoon we thought the roads must be getting drifted full. By four o'clock it was dark and still snowing just as hard, with the wind howling unabated, so we closed in for the night, thinking the storm would let up by the next day.

The storm rages on

We went to bed early, knowing we had plenty of wood and coal in. The woodsheds and coalbin were almost connected with the house and both were nearly full. We went to sleep with the hewn frame of the house jarring from the force of the wind, but our sleep was undisturbed by fear.

The storm was still going on when we awakened in the morning. There was now no sound of snow against the window panes, as they were already deeply encrusted with the wet snow of the day before, which had now frozen solid. This morning was just as dark as the day before and it seemed as though it would never come daylight.

Edwin and I went in to see what had become of Edward. I opened the door of his room and found that the bed and everything in the room was covered with from six to ten inches of snow, which had drifted through a small, triangular hole in the window pane. There was no Edward to be seen until, by us poking around at the covers, the snow began to crack open and presently up popped a woolly black head and Edward looked like a little black chicken coming out of a shell.

When he saw the snow his eyes danced with delight. As he was already dressed, except for his boots, which stood beside the kitchen stove, he was quickly ready to go with us to the barn.

We opened the kitchen door to go outside and found it packed with deep snow, almost to the top, so we pushed the snow out and climbed over it and went to the woodshed to get our shovels. The snow lay waist-deep until we got to the end of the spruce trees, but from there to the barn it was still mostly all bare ground because of the terrific gale that was blowing. As we opened the small door to go into the barn my brother's sou'wester hat went straight up and has never been seen since.

The gale takes a hat

The barnyard was fairly clear of snow, except where it had drifted up against the barn and the cow stables, where we had to tunnel about twenty-four feet to get to the door of the cow stables. When we finished, it was about nine o'clock and the cattle were all calling for feed and water.

As Edward and I walked in front of the corn house we heard a low, muffled, grinding sound. We walked inside, over the snowdrifts that had almost filled the corn house, and found that Edwin had dug out the cornsheller and was shelling corn for the chickens. Upstairs in the corn house were bins filled with grain, a workbench with tools lying on it, and all was covered with snow that had blown up the stairs and settled down everywhere. Each tool on the workbench was plainly outlined under the blanket of snow.

Up in the rafters and cross beams were rows and rows of snowbirds, wise little things they were to find the grain bins. From under a Norway spruce tree near the house came a clucking sound which called for investigation. We forced our way under the snow-laden branches to the trunk of the tree. There, in a little round nest made of the spruce branchlets and completely free of snow, was a brown hen and one newly hatched chick. We immediately moved both to a warm place in the house. We named this little ball of fluff Blizzard.

During all this time the same driving sleet and snow were coming from the Northwest, an unusual quarter. The gale was so strong that the windward sides of the old rail fences were scoured down to new wood. The mercury continued to hover at about seven above zero.

The drifts were becoming immense around the house and buildings. The roads and fences were all drifted under, except in the bleak spots where even the brown fields were exposed to the force of the wind. Where the snow had blown from the cleared lands into the woods, it drifted trees under to a depth of from twenty to thirty feet. As the snow later thawed and froze it bent and broke many of the trees by its weight.

One of the most unusual things about the storm was the darkness of the days, an even darkness that did not vary for hours. All of us kept commenting about it being the worst storm we had ever seen. The wind blew around the tenant house so violently that it left the house standing in a yard of brown grass, while about twenty feet to the north was a drift twenty-four feet deep, covering three apple trees.

Wednesday was very much the same, and on Thursday the storm finally broke. During all this time we had seen no one else, not even our nearest neighbors. John Wing, our elderly mail carrier, who always made his ten-mile daily journey on foot, was unable to deliver the mail for over a week. This meant we could get no word from my mother and sister, marooned by the storm at Leather Hill, or they from us.

Neither could we enjoy our usual evening reading of the New York Times or the Poughkeepsie Daily Eagle. But even if we boys had the daily newspapers we would have been too worn out by our day's work of hay foddering and snow shoveling to keep awake long enough to read them.

Wednesday night, the wind died down, and by Thursday morning it began to grow lighter. All the land that had been swept clean of snow by the high winds was now covered with an even white coat. Before noon the storm broke and, as the sky cleared, we realized just how heavy a blanket of snow had fallen. Since the previous Sunday night we had heard no whistle of any train, nor did we until the following Monday.

When my mother and sister finally returned home several days after the storm ended, there was great rejoicing and we had our experiences to compare.

Ten days after the storm, the drift on those three apple trees near the tenant house had alternately thawed and frozen. On it could be found the lot of Montana horses that had been recently shipped in, drowsing on top of one of the apple trees that had been drifted under, the limbs now showing above the snow. Eventually, this beautiful, young Baldwin tree was mashed flat to the ground.

Aftermath of the "Blizzard of '88"

I am glad to have been old enough to remember this snowstorm, for as long as I lived in New York State it was used as the measuring stick for all large storms. I have only to close my eyes now to bring back a mental picture of our home when The Ridge endured the largest snow storm of record, now called the Blizzard of '88.

Benson Lossing sketch: "The First House Erected
on Quaker Hill, Dutchess County."

Chapter IX
ROADS FROM OUR HOUSE

On the road to Dover Plains, the village down in the valley, a gentle slope led to the top of what we called Nerbas's Hill. This was the nearest hill suitable for coasting, and we children used it for that purpose.

The first part was quite steep and made a sharp turn before extending in a long, straight line to the foot of the hill and across a bridge over Wells Brook. This stream came from natural wells about three miles further in the woods.

Wells Brook

The wells were seven in number, and worn in the rock, one being sixty feet deep. The surface around them sloped toward the edge and was covered with pine needles. This made them very dangerous to approach. Years earlier a member of a party slipped and fell into the well, and it required the services of a diver to recover his body.

One summer's day my cousin and I vowed we would cut our names in the rock at the edge of the water line in one of these wells. We made a ladder of ropes that were an inch thick and tied them to countless saplings back from the edge of the wells. Then we lowered our ladder about thirty feet to the water, where there was a flat rock we could stand on.

We stood on this slippery rock and carved our names on the wall. At the upper side of the well was the waterfall of the brook, plunging down into the black water and overflowing through the immense fissure in the rock to the next well below.

Carving our names in stone

While we were working with our heavy hammer and chisels, a ray of sunlight guided us in our carving, but before we had finished it became almost too dark to see. A thunderstorm was coming up from the west, and although the roar of the waterfall drowned out the thunder, we could tell the storm was coming on account of the darkness.

My cousin looked very pale, and if I looked the way I felt, I must have been pale, also. It took us longer than we expected, and we were chilled through before we were finally finished. Completing our three-hour task, we climbed up the ladder to find the storm was veering to the north, and it did not reach us.

I don't know what our mothers would have thought had they known where we spent the afternoon. We had always been warned about the wells—a relative of ours had been with the man who was lost there. We called it a successful adventure, and the names could be seen ever afterward in the morning sunlight, from the slope toward the well.

Nerbas's Hill had a "watchtower," as we children named a big flat rock which stood on the curve where one of us always stood to warn of approaching sleigh teams. There was a rotation of lookouts, and we each took our turn.

In steering our sleighs around this curve, we always wore out the right heel of our shoes and rubbers. We later devised a remedy for this by using some tin and string as a right heel guard. Skidding around the curve with increasing speed, we would ride to the foot of the hill and across the bridge, then along a level stretch for a ways.

All this took about fifteen seconds compared to five minutes for the return climb.

At the left of the road above the bridge was the Piper house, which stood on the Nerbas property. The Pipers were colored, and what I remember about them was that Fanny Piper, their little girl, had diphtheria one winter.

The Piper family and illness

During this illness, Fanny's mother came up to our place for a bundle of clothes that my mother gave her. My mother placed the clothes at a great distance from our house, laying them on the snow. Mrs. Piper came and took the bundle home with her.

The word diphtheria frightened us, and even long afterward we were almost afraid to pass the Piper house.

About a quarter of a mile beyond the bridge and around the curve in the road—where another glimpse of the valley could be caught—lived Mrs. Murphy and her sons Charlie and George. Mr. Murphy had been killed in the Civil War.

The Murphys

The lot where the house stood was considerably below the road, which made it sheltered from the wind. North of this house stood a little hovel for their one cow, with a chicken house adjoining. To the south was a potato patch and a garden. A small meadow afforded hay for the cow.

Charlie Murphy was a cripple. his legs and arms being terribly deformed. His skin seemed to be drawn over his frame, and he was hunchbacked besides. You could hardly understand what he said, he was so tongue-tied. In his stiff hands he carried a cane. He had the sweetest expression on his face that I have ever seen. His eyes. a deep violet blue. seemed to shine with joy. You could always tell where Charlie had been by his tracks. because in the dust of the road the track would be in a sweeping circle. His poor feet were so deformed that he could not wear shoes.

Charlie would come up to us with a basket of clothes his mother had laundered, a distance of over a mile. When he arrived with the laundry, he would smile and try to tell all about the adventure of his journey. On Christmas morning, our first trip was to take a basket of cakes to Charlie Murphy.

George Murphy was a well-built man, an excellent woodchopper and worker in general. He had washed-out, expressionless eyes and was always chewing tobacco. Mrs. Murphy was short and skinny but had large bones, and her forearms were extremely long. She wore her black hair in a high twist, and her yellowed skin was very much wrinkled on her face and neck. She had great strength and endurance.

A hard-working woman

During spring housecleaning time, Mrs. Murphy could beat carpets and scrub floors all day, then walk home at night. When away from home she always wore large brass earrings shaped like Bartlett pears. And as her head was slightly palsied, these earrings were constantly swinging as she scrubbed and hurried around. While she worked, she talked a continuous stream, about her work, her home, and Charlie.

Some years afterward we heard of Mrs. Murphy's remarriage. The happy bridegroom was none other than Zachariah Story, one of our former hired men, who now owned a small place down the mountain near Ann Wing's.

Zachariah took his bride to his comfortable house, which was nestled in a pear orchard and surrounded by miniature meadows in the woods. The "setting room" floor was covered with a warm rag carpet and some small rag rugs. In front of the fireplace, which had been bricked up, was a square woodstove, with a cast iron urn on top. Back against the chimney was the woodbox, its sides covered with chintz, a ruffle around the bottom.

On each side of the stove was a Boston rocking chair, upholstered in a red pattern, with lace tidies adorning the back and arms. On one side of the room was a table with a red tablecloth and a kerosene lamp in the center. A piece of red flannel was in the lamp.

On the mantle stood a steeple clock with a panel under the dial, adorned with a painting of an old mill and a stone bridge. Chromes of the Civil War hung on the walls. The air was full of the songs of canaries in cages that hung in front of each window. On the window shelves were pots with red geraniums blooming and pink primroses.

Later, the old Murphy house burned to the ground.

Further on, the road ran along a meadow sloping to the east, and beyond that it followed a large and very stony pasture with a spring house in the middle of it. Beside the spring house was a small, crooked old oak that shaded the roof and helped keep the water cool. The spring house was used for cooling milk by setting the cans in the water. It was inhabited by some very green frogs. Often, when one opened the door to the spring house, frogs would be sitting on the whitewashed sills, entirely dried off and apparently sleepy.

The spring house and my poem

This spring once inspired me to poetic thinking as I sat there, stirring the milk to cool it. (Our own spring had gone dry at the time.) I called my poem "Work, Nothing but Work," and it went something like this:

Five in the morning and up with a will,
Turn out the cattle and then feed old Bill.
Down to the milk spring, puddle and bog,
Wiggling tadpole and sleepy frog.

Sit and stir till the milk gets cool,
Nothing for thought but the dark, black pool.
When off in the east comes broad daylight
And in with the milk cans with all your might.

*Nothing
but work*

Down through the lane with a rattle and bang,
Perched on a lily a bobwhite sang.
Out through the gate with a terrible clatter,
Wheels flying round and nothing the matter.

Down to the creamery, never a spill,
Though coming back it was all uphill.
Wife in the pantry, without e'er a mutter,
A-scouring the pans and a-working the butter.

Wears an expression, worn-out and tired,
She seldom was seen and never admired.
"How about breakfast. Is that ready yet?"
For Johnnie and Jimmie and little Annette.

Down in the valley, beyond hill and dell,
At the death of old Pendergrast they're tolling the
bell.
He was milking his cow and he died with a jerk,
For his life and religion were nothing but work.

Beyond this stony pasture we went up a short hill and
around a curve—a place always drifted full of snow in
the winter. A short distance beyond, three pine trees
stood in a yard. Back of these and further in was a
house belonging to a man by the name of Pugglesly.

This house was said to be haunted by the ghost of Margery Whittleson, who had lived here for many years before the Puggleslys came.

Before her death, Margery had chosen Poughkeepsie for her burial place, but when she died it was decided to bury her in the local cemetery in the valley. On the day of the funeral, however, when the horses were turned toward the valley they balked and would not go. They were perfectly willing to go toward Poughkeepsie, though. In fact, they insisted, and old Margery got her burial wish after all.

Ever afterward the house was considered haunted.

A little further on, going down toward the valley, was the house of Bat O'Hearn, who had bushy brown whiskers. The house stood in an apple orchard, about a hundred feet from the highway. It was a story-and-a-half, whitewashed, with a big stone chimney at one end. The bulge of the brick oven showed plainly on the outside.

Bat O'Hearn's old house

The floors of the house were almost worn through, for it had been an old house before the O'Hearns moved in. They and their three sons and a daughter had added to the general wear and tear. But worn as the floor was, it was always scrubbed as white as could be.

The paint on the rooms had the original old dark blue, and many of the original seven-by-nine panes were still in the sash. Much of the old glass was so imperfect it was hard to see through.

In front of the door were large slate stones for a step. A little beyond to the south was an immense willow tree. Below the tree, at the foot of a steep bank ran the Dover Stone Church brook, deriving its name from a grotto formed in the rocks by the washing of the brook for ages.

About two miles below O'Hearn's, this grotto gave the appearance of the Gothic entrance to a church

107

when one approached from the lower side. Upon entering the "church," one would find the interior, about twenty-four feet square, with a well-proportioned Gothic roof and a fissure in the ridge of the ceiling where the sky showed through. A splendid growth of ferns hung down from over the edge.

A natural grotto like a church

In the far end of the grotto was a long rock standing on end. It had evidently dropped from a crevice in the ceiling and formed an almost perfect pulpit. Back of this "pulpit" was a waterfall, from which flowed a brook around the gravelly floor of the "church."

The approach to this place from the village was through two gates and down a grassy lane. The path forded a stream and led up to a small grassy plateau which was used as a picnic ground, for which it was an ideal place. The ground was gravelly and dry, though kept green by the shade of trees and by the cool mist occasionally coming down the canyon from the waterfall in the grotto.

Above the picnic ground was the beginning of the canyon leading to the grotto. Along the canyon's south side was the path, made of black cinders, to the right of which were high rocks. In many places, these rocks overhung the path and rose to heights of forty feet. They were beautifully green with moss and ferns.

Just below O'Hearn's a little spring bubbled out of the soft slate, flowing most of the year but disappearing in very dry weather. Below this spring the Dover Stone Church brook crossed the highway twice within a very short distance.

Dover Stone Church Brook

The first bridge was rather high above the water, built on the slope of the hill. Descending from this bridge, the traveler came to a level section of the road just a little higher than the brook, which spread out here with a gravelly bottom beyond a grassy spot. One could drive through the brook and down the stream a way and let the horses drink, then drive out of the brook onto the road, around a curve to a second bridge.

At the side of the road on this curve was a prominent slate rock, the spot where my sister's phaeton was dashed when Fannie and Katie took a notion to run away. Beyond the second bridge and quite high above the bank was the spot we termed "the dumping place," because it was here that Fannie shied at the snowbank and backed us off, dumping us in the raspberry bushes.

Right after the second bridge was another small bridge over a stream that was dry most of the year. Then the road entered the woods, mostly tall and straight chestnut trees. Soon after entering the woods, the Richmond place was to be seen on the left side of the road. This was a log house that had been covered with lapboard siding. It had a window at the end toward the road, two windows and a door on the south side. A stone step was in front of the door, and there was a small gate of poles, generally in tumbledown condition.

Two or three parts of wagons were always standing around, and a skinny horse was kept in a hovel on the east end of the house. The garden and potato patch fence was in keeping with the gate: built of poles nailed to the post and some wire and a few boards and a patched-up pair of bars. Beyond was a beautiful little meadow with a few oak stumps and timothy grass growing rank.

A brook meandered through this meadow in the summer. As the meadow was sheltered by the woods and some very tall oak trees, it was one of the first places where grass became green in the spring.

Beside the road in front of the Richmond house was an old chestnut tree which had been pretty well wrecked by ice storms, and yet it still served for a tie post. Staples and iron rings were driven into one side of it, and on that side the horses had stripped the bark away.

A very cute bulldog lived there, and one spring he stood out by the road wagging his tail when we came driving along. My sister called from the wagon, "You sweetsie, dearie, little pupsie wupsie," when suddenly the window flew up and a rough-looking girl stuck out her head, grinned, and shouted, "Don't swaller the dog, quite!" Above her head, one of the panes was gone, replaced by a sack filled with straw.

Beyond here we drove along a stretch of road that was always muddy in the spring. Then we went up a short hill with a big oak tree to the right. There followed a level piece of road, flanked on the south by an alder swamp.

The cart road

We then started down what was termed "the cart road," a very steep hill at first. The steep pitch soon merged into a gentle grade with high rocks on the right. Under their shelter were beautiful ferns, watered by the dripping from the rocks.

At the turn of the road was a group of large oaks, and beyond them opened a view across a hillside pasture toward the valley and the Connecticut mountains. Rounding this curve, the road led gently down a hill until it came to another steep place.

At the left were domelike gray rocks, and beyond was a green plateau where a small red house stood in an apple orchard. Here lived elderly Mr. and Mrs. Leighton and their daughters, Katie and Lizzie. This was a chunkily built family, with the exception of Liz, who was more slender, and also more pouty.

Mrs. Leighton's dog

They had a big shepherd dog, I remember, because we shot him once with our air gun, which made him jump up and squeal. Mrs. Leighton immediately came to the door, but by that time we had driven past and were looking the other way.

At the foot of the hill was the main highway leading from New York to Pittsfield. Across this road was a typi-

cal village schoolhouse, painted white and accommodating about fifty pupils. The schoolmaster was Mr.
Perry, a large man of about sixty, with a finely shaped
head and features. He always wore a Prince Albert coat
and dark trousers, a white shirt and black bow tie. He
was beloved by everyone who knew him.

*Mr. Perry,
the old
schoolmaster*

My brother, who attended the school, once modeled
a four-inch high head of Mr. Perry, and also some
smaller ones of two inches. From the molds he cast
one for every student who wished one, and Mr. Perry
was wonderfully pleased.

Mr. Perry boarded up the road in the Louisa Belden
Inn, at the foot of Plymouth Hill. This was one of the
old hostelries of Colonial design. It had a big tub of
running water near the roadside, under a willow tree,
where horses could drink before starting up the hill.
The inn had a long, deep veranda, paved with flat
stones where you entered the lower rooms. Because
it was on a hillside, guests could walk from this veranda right onto the ground.

The parlors and dining rooms had heavy Colonial
doors, grained to imitate oak. The driveway was of
gravel taken from the river, and there were maple and
elm trees in the yard, through which could be seen the
red stables.

Steve Cooper's house was the first one from our place
on the Coopertown Road, a one-way road with occasional turnouts between the rocks and mud holes.
Steve was a tall, raw-boned mountaineer with bushy
whiskers and long, coarse brown hair.

*Cooper's,
site of a
murder*

According to local legend, he and his son went up
one night to the Corners (called "town") and got drunk.
The son was, at the time, about sixteen. It seems someone asked him if he could knock in the head of a barrel
with his head. When he attempted this feat he was
unaware a grindstone had been substituted for the

barrel head. The resulting injury made him an imbecile.

Some time after that, his father ordered him off his place. He came back several times, each time being ordered away. The last time, as he put his foot on the doorstone, his father shot him dead. As with fourteen other cases of murder in that section within thirty years, the murderer went free. It was through the influence of a disreputable man who, for forty-three years, was our congressman.

Steve Cooper had a brother, much shorter in stature, but his whiskers were bushier and his hair longer. He peddled huckleberries and blackberries, driving a team of black jackasses hitched to a small square box wagon filled with tin pails of berries. One day he passed our house and sold us some huckleberries. His face was badly skinned and he was teetering on his feet.

In reply to our question as to how he had skinned his face, he squealed in his high voice, "I fell out the wagon and don't know how it happened. I was parfactly sober."

McIntyre's cottage

The next house above Cooper's on the Coopertown Road belonged to Mrs. McIntyre. Her husband, long since dead, had left her his little clearing in the woods with sufficient land for cultivation, pasture for four cows and a little garden. In the rear of her house was a mountain brook.

Living with her was her son, who was tall, as she was. One summer a blacksmith persuaded him to accompany him to his home state, North Dakota. To pay her son's way back, Mrs. McIntyre had to sell all four cows. The trip cured him of his wanderlust, and he was content to stay home ever afterward. Later, he worked in a sawmill and went by the name "Gooseneck."

Beyond Mrs. McIntyre's lived Joe Dennis, a man with a well-proportioned body, strong arms and handsome features. But, when Joe was a child, his legs were cut off above the ankles by a mowing machine, so he went through life walking on his knees which he had padded with leather.

Joe Dennis

It was wonderful to observe his cheerful patience as he went his way doing all the work on his little farm in the woods, even driving a team to the village to get his horses shod. At the blacksmith's one day, he was warned about getting too close to a certain horse's heels.

"Oh, he'll kick over me," Joe replied with laugh.

"Milton Ferry and Horse Boat," by Benson Lossing.

Chapter X
VISITS AND VACATION

Visits to Aunt Fannie Titus's family at Titusville were wonderful, both in anticipation and in reality. When we heard a visit was in prospect we would hug each other and kick up our heels.

There were three roads to Aunt Fannie's: The longest was by way of the turnpike; another was through Mansfield, then Verbank, across Freedom Plains and over Van Benschoten's hill; the third and shortest was the "back road" that branched off the Freedom Plains road. We seldom took the turnpike to go to Titusville because it was such a roundabout way. When going there in winter, we tried to avoid taking the Freedom Plains road, which in that season was terrible. This road

Titusville visits

115

was perfectly straight for three miles, a windswept plain of frozen horse tracks and with ice in the ruts.

In good weather, we preferred the Freedom Plains road, and if we wanted to visit on the way with Aunt Betty and cousin John Buck we took that turnoff on the back road. The Buck's white-painted, green-shuttered house was up a driveway about five hundred feet and stood in a grove of locust and Norway spruce trees. The red carriage house was across the lane, near the house, and further back up the hill was the brown barn.

The Freedom Plains road

Our arrival at the Bucks, at about eleven o'clock, was necessarily unannounced, as those were the days before the telephone. Immediately after we got there, Cousin Irene came in and my Aunt Betty asked her if she had put wood in the kitchen stove. Soon we heard a prolonged squawk from the direction of the henhouse and my older sister and I looked at each other understandingly. Sure enough, we would have a delicious chicken dinner about one o'clock.

After dinner and a visit with Aunt Betty we proceeded on our way to Aunt Fannie's. Before we got there, we passed the Presbyterian church. We called it "Presbyteri-an" because the "an" was separate from the rest of the word in the gilt lettering on the big, black, oval board up in the gable. A few hundred feet farther on was a small group of houses and a blacksmith's shop. The weathervane on the shop was Gabriel, lying on his stomach, blowing his trumpet. This lifesize figure was made of wood and painted white.

We would arrive at Aunt Fannie's about four o'clock. Driving in the gate we could hear shuffling and scuffling on the broad veranda, and running to us from under the wisteria vine came cousins Helen, Adele and Annette, grinning from ear to ear. They soon were followed by Uncle Robert, smoking his pipe and greeting us warmly. Aunt Fannie, her lovely face framed in brown curls, would be standing to meet us as we drove under the porte-cochere.

Aunt Fannie's

In 1876, my father, mother, oldest sister and brother had gone to the Centennial fair at Philadelphia, and the two weeks our family was away, my younger sister and I spent with our Aunt Fannie. My sister and I had longed to go to the fair, but we were too young. We were told we could go to the next one, which pacified us. I did not then realize I would be 104 years old by then. What I remember best about that stay at Aunt Fannie's was going across the immense lawn, dotted with groups of Norway spruce trees, to the croquet ground and hunting in the hot sun for croquet balls under the hedge of arbor vitae that lined the inside of the front stone wall. I was fortunate if I could make a trip across the lawn without being knocked down and rolled over by Nero, the big, black Newfoundland dog, friendly but rough.

It seemed that thousands of trips were made across that lawn to the silver ice-water pitcher in the darkened dining room. If colored Ann or Aunt Fannie were not there to pour the water for us, we were obliged to stand on a chair and tip the heavy pitcher for ourselves.

Ice water and lawns

It was a very happy sight to see Uncle Robert coming home from the factory late in the afternoon because every child loved him. He would be smiling and laughing and I used to sit and look at him and think he was just perfect.

The woolen mills owned by "Elias Titus and Sons," of which Uncle Robert was one of the sons, were in Titusville on Wappingers Creek. The creek was lined with beech and sycamore trees and elms, and the water from it was diverted through a long raceway and flume to the waterwheel of the mill. The mill was a long, three-story, wooden building, painted yellow ochre, and it stood at the foot of what they called "factory hill." In front of this mill the road crossed a picturesque bridge shadowed by an immense willow tree and ending in the factory meadow.

We also looked forward to visiting my mother's cousins, George Sweet and his sister Elizabeth, who lived at Washington Hollow, about eleven miles from our home. When we made these annual or semi-annual visits, they were kept short so as not to tire the sickly Elizabeth. Mother spoke of it as "going to auntie's," but we called it "going to Cousin George's."

George and Elizabeth lived on a road branching off from the main road. To the left, as one drove in, were low meadows. To the right was a long row of locust trees, and beyond them meadows rose to the west, dotted with apple trees. At the end of the row of locust trees was a horse block, built in the picket fence, and beyond that a gate to the driveway leading into the yard. On the opposite side of the road from the driveway a gate led into the pasture and just inside this gate was an immense black walnut tree, its branches trimmed level on the underside by the browsing of cattle and horses. Whenever we arrived, a young horse always seemed to be trotting up to this gate to greet us, looking over with his nose quivering and making a half-whinnying sound. The gentle treatment these horses received was reflected in their gentle eyes.

A short distance up the driveway stood the house, long and low, a story-and-a-half, facing the south. Across the driveway, steps led down into the garden, where old-fashioned flowers grew along the gravelled paths. At one end of this garden was a long grape arbor, hung in season with beautiful round, blue-black Concord grapes. The Sweet house had a small Colonial porch, with slim round columns. Its four or five steps led to seats on both sides of the porch, and the six-panelled door had a brass knocker and a large keyhole. Toward the west end of this house was a long porch, extending the full length of the kitchen and the room adjoining.

We walked up the front steps, clapped the knocker,

and stood whispering until Cousin Elizabeth opened the door. She always looked so happy to see us and ushered us into the living room. This was a good-sized, sunny room with a black mantelpiece. Between the two south windows was Cousin George's desk, a square, flat affair like a table with drawers at each side. Beyond the window and between it and the kitchen door stood a tall, dark mahogany secretary with curved legs and claw feet.

Mother and Cousin Elizabeth would talk over the congenial subject of the Sweets in general and we young ones would sit and listen with interest. In younger days, Cousin Elizabeth several times had horses run away with her, having been thrown from their backs as well as from wagons when driving. Her descriptions of these accidents made it seem to us she had been cracked all to pieces, several bones being broken.

These injuries had stiffened Cousin Elizabeth's body and limbs to the extent that she was quite round-shouldered, walking with short steps, head bent forward. Still, her hair was a most beautiful golden brown, not a gray hair showing, even at sixty. It was worn high on her head, held up with a "Spanish" comb. Her face was rather thin and pale, her eyes large and brown and her expression the kindest one could ever expect to see.

Cousin Elizabeth's courage

Cousin Elizabeth took her afflictions as a joke, making the stories of her accidents most ridiculous. She walked with little steps around the room as she talked, going into her bedroom and out again, generally holding her handkerchief under one arm. If we stayed for a noon meal it seemed to take forever for her to get it ready. She first moved the square, slim-legged, cherry table out from the wall to the center of the room. After the white cloth was spread, the dishes came out one by one. They were the best white china and were brought to the table by individual trips from the chimney closet beside the fireplace.

No one ever knew how Cousin Elizabeth finally managed to get the dinner all together, between her stops for quaint conversation and her wanderings back and forth, but I have recollections of delicious chicken and everything that goes with it. My mother would be saying all this time, "Now, Elizabeth, don't go to any trouble."

After a while, Cousin George would slowly come in, shake hands all around and look straight at each of us with his dark blue eyes. He had an exceedingly slow manner of speech. Sometimes his conversation would be about old times, and sometimes about the county fair, of which he was treasurer. Or he might ask my eldest sister, a horse lover, if she did not want to see "El Capitan," a beautiful black Percheron stallion he had exhibited there.

Among my earliest memories were the stories told by Cousin George, then about sixty years of age. He was a tall man with a very high nose and a straight mouth and he wore side whiskers. Cousin George had gone to California in the days of '49, by way of Panama, and had engaged in mining. On account of his father's death, he was forced to return to New York and take care of his mother, to whom he was devoted.

Cousin George telling stories

One day when we were walking with Cousin George by an outcropping of rock near the main road north of the house, he told us about his Uncle Silas, who had rafted lumber down the Hudson from Fort Edward. My great-uncle Silas once had dreamed of coming home on a raft of logs and grounding on these very rocks.

I imagine that same story caused me later to dream of landing from a steamship or a sailing vessel between the two cherry trees near our barn.

In summertime, we took vacations, and one July day when I was about four years old the whole family started off for Fire Island, the summer resort and bathing place on the Long Island shore. When our train reached New York City we went to the Grand Central Hotel, but our baggage had accidentally been sent on ahead.

Fire Island

The weather was terribly hot, and without our baggage we had nothing to wear but warm flannel clothing that had been comfortable when we had started in the cool morning. My younger sister and I were wearing blue plaid flannel kilts and Scotch caps with ribbons in the back, high black shoes and stockings the color of graham bread.

That night, my brother and I slept on a mattress on the floor, and in the morning they found me with the shell of a loaf of bread. Somehow I had acquired the bread, which I kept by my side on the mattress. I had dug into the loaf until nothing was left but the shell, with a round hole where my hand had gone in. This seemed to amuse the family for years.

Our next stop was Flushing, Long Island, where we had a three-hour wait in the heat and humidity until the train for Hunter's Point came. Sitting in my hot blue flannel dress, I leaned against what I thought was my father and fell asleep. Next thing I knew another man was looking down at me and laughing.

Then came the boat trip, my first. I remember peering into the engine room and smelling the steam, then stepping over the side-wheel shaft, which was turning above the deck. We approached the bay side of the island, and in front of Sammelton's Hotel the boat turned around and landed.

The boat trip and boardwalk

We disembarked and walked about seventy-five yards down the boardwalk to the hotel, entering through a broad hall that went right through the building and was covered with manila matting. There I saw Mr. Sammelton, who was tall and thin and had narrow, gray chin whiskers and sharp features. He gave us rooms on the bay side of the hotel. My father did not stay with us, leaving to manage business affairs, perhaps in the city.

The room I was in with my mother and younger sister was not very large. It was furnished with a set of ivory-painted furniture with blue and red roses on it, and the windows were screened with cotton mosquito netting. From these windows we could look out on the bay and see the clam sloops and other boats moored to the dock along the shore. In the morning one of the first sounds to be heard was the grinding of the tackle blocks as these boats were making sail for the day's run.

That sound and the memory of the salt air have always lingered delightfully in my mind. I never forgot the smell of the manila matting and the Pond's Extract used for mosquito bites. Mosquitoes were practically a new experience. They were thick on the outside of the netting on the windows, which swayed back and *The hotel* forth in the breeze. Stretched along the ocean side of the long hotel was the covered board porch with big wooden rocking chairs with splint bottoms scattered along the whole distance. As we went out the lobby door on the ocean side, immediately to the right was the barber shop with a jet-black barber who liked to make grimaces at me.

Walking along the porch some distance, we passed the windows of the two hotel parlors. Beyond these on the end of the hotel was a door from the large parlor leading onto a square, covered pavilion. On the other side was a barroom, shooting gallery and bowling alley. From the pavilion, running toward the ocean, was a wide boardwalk. On the pavilion's ocean side was the dining room.

Beside the dining room was a tall ice water tank, painted blue with a tin cup chained to it. The dining room was a large, square affair with tall windows divided into small panes. The room had round and oblong tables with yellow legs. We had delicious things to eat at this place. There were bluefish, clams and all kinds of seafood, and only Mother's restraining hand kept us from eating all we wanted. I remember a waitress coming down the long dining room with a tray full of dishes. Then a dish of peas fell off the tray, and the waitress just kicked the whole mess under a table.

Just beyond the hotel were four or five cottages. In one of these was Mrs. Hatch, a cousin of my mother's, and her son, Artie. Like the boardwalk, these cottages stood on posts about three feet above the sand, as heavy storms had been known to wash in on them.

Also on Fire Island was a tall lighthouse, a bathing pavilion and boardwalks. The boardwalk from the hotel to the ocean was over a quarter-mile long and was not covered from the sun except at a halfway place that had a board roof and seats. Going out to the beach was a lovely walk across the sand, but very hot and tiresome if the sun were strong. Strange to say, there were many hissing adders on the sand. These were dark, gray snakes about fifteen inches long, with flat heads and thick bodies. We could see them from the platform.

Hissing adders on the sand

Near the ocean, the platform went up a grade and over the sand dunes to a pavilion and two rows of weather-beaten bathing houses on the shore. This was a splendid bathing beach, with the breakers rolling in, and we young ones in our bathing suits spent much of the time in the water and on the beach. We would let the surf wash up on our feet and then run back and play with wooden buckets and shovels in the sand.

My older sister and my brother would float or swim in the surf. Mother never went in, but cousin Mary Ann Ferris, in her blue flannel bathing suit trimmed with white braid, would. Her suit had a sailor collar, a heavy, full skirt that came to her knees, and under that were bloomers shirred at the ankles. Her hat was of straw, going up to a peak in the center, with a slimpsy broad brim bent down over her ears and tied with a cord. All the ladies wore similar suits.

On this beach one day I was sailing a large cigar box boat in the water and nearby another boy was trying to sail a small one, but his would not float and rolled over and over. He became very angry and jealous, stomped mine to pieces and ran away.

A crushed cigar box boat

In the evening, the parlors of the hotel were at first used for the entertainment of the children. This consisted of dancing and a performance by a ventriloquist, who pretended to be driving a wagon and running over animals, imitating their voices. Soon I spied that boy, who was much older and larger than I, sitting beside the door watching the other children dance.

I decided it was a good time to punish him for what he had done to me, so I bottled up all the steam I could muster, walked in front of him and hit him in the nose. There was a buzz of mothers and a lot of explaining, and I felt vindicated.

A punched nose for punishment

Another older boy there was very kind to me. He showed me how to bowl with little balls, and I followed him all over. He would let a mosquito bite him, and while it sucked the blood he would clip the end of its body off with a pair of sharp scissors. The mosquito would keep on sucking, the blood running out on the boy's hand.

One day at the pavilion I noticed the bar and the men at it drinking foamy things that looked good to me, so I went in and asked for a drink. The bartender seemed flabbergasted and laughed, and I walked out, puzzled.

At the hotel there was a widower with his little son and daughter. He didn't know how to fix their hair, and one very hot day he came out with the little girl's pigtails wound around tight the whole length with a ribbon, so they stuck right out straight. Later, some of the ladies took pity on the children and helped him.

A German man there taught his eight-year-old boy to swim by putting him on a plank and swimming out into deep water with him, the boy yelling all the while at the top of his lungs. Then the father would suddenly turn the plank over. It was no time before the boy learned to swim and enjoyed it.

German swimming lessons

In the evening the ladies would sit on the ocean side of the hotel in the big rocking chairs, fighting mosquitoes. One lady had leggings made of stiff brown paper to cover her legs.

Much to my disappointment, I never got to climb up the lighthouse, as it was quite a long walk through the sand dunes and a long way up to the light. My brother and sister made the trip and later described it to me.

At the end of our stay on Fire Island my father returned for us and we packed up and went home with a collection of clam, oyster and mussel shells.

Study of a country church by Benson Lossing.

Chapter XI
CHURCH, MEETING HOUSES AND DUTCHESS PIKE

When I was a boy, our church, Grace Episcopal, was relatively new. It was boxlike, with a Sunday school in the ell, and a large pair of stiff sliding doors between the church and the Sunday school.

Our church

The pews were of black walnut and butternut, treated with linseed oil, and they always smelled like it. The seats had red cushions and both aisles were covered with green carpet. The vestibule was covered with a rope matting, and the outside porch was plain, with five steps in front and no roof. The building was painted gray.

In the rear was a long shed for teams. In the yard were some maple trees two inches in diameter and ten feet high. The roof was adorned with a belfry about ten sizes too small for the church. I think the bell was a second-hand one from a locomotive.

(I'm reminded of what an Englishman remarked about our bells around the time of the Revolution: "British bells said 'King George, roast beef! King George, roast beef!' while American bells said, 'Continental Congress, Continental Congress!'")

The church had two memorial windows of fair enough quality stained glass. The other windows were of very ordinary stained glass which cast a weird, seasick green hue on faces that were really a jelly red; to others the light gave a jaundiced effect, and to still others a speckled blue or a doleful purple cast. As if that were not enough, the heat from the noonday sun made beads of perspiration run down these faces of variegated hues.

Stained glass and sunlight

The design in the large memorial window above the chancel rail was of two angels in the clouds worshiping a gilded cross radiating light. Their figures were unmistakably Dutch. They wore heavy purple and blue robes with sandaled feet. Their wings were large and stiff and with their apparent weight I often wondered how they ever flew.

This window was on the south end of the church and so made it bad for the eyes of the congregation with the scorching midday sun shining through so the minister looked like a black silhouette. Around the Gothic arch in front of the chancel rail, one could just discern the words, "The Lord is in His Holy Temple, let all the earth keep silence before Him."

The rope from the belfry came down outside the doors to the interior of the church, and when the sexton tolled the bell he stood off to one side, back of these doors. The rope dragged at an acute angle across the scuttle of the belfry, making a rasping sound before each peal, and with every pull the sexton's coattails would bob back and forth from behind the door.

The Merritt girl always came late to service. She was fat, about fifteen, and would walk up the aisle briskly, slide into her pew, plump down immediately on her knees, then wiggle against the back of the seat. She wore a starched white dress with blue sash, white stockings, squeaky shoes, and a broad-brimmed white straw hat with a wreath of white bullseye daisies. She seemed to feel very superior, and maybe she was, but to us she seemed just plain pudgy.

Our little congregation

Directly in front of us sat Mr. and Mrs. McAllister, a dear old English couple. Poor Mr. McAllister would doze during long sermons. Perhaps it was the glare of the light.

Next to them in the same pew were the Haight girls, lovely sisters. They had another sister, who for a long time was too ill to attend church, and we always asked how she was. The answer was always, "She's gainin'." For a year and a half we asked the question and the answer was always the same.

In the next pew was the John D. Wing family, summer residents who later built a fine home on a nearby hill. Their money was made in the meat-packing business, and they were just ignorant enough to be snobby. After the minister had made the congregation believe the former church was "fast going to decay," the Wings had furnished a large part of the money, land for the site, and an architect, to build this church. It was the homeliest conglomeration one could imagine. Apparently there was not quite enough money to finish the steeple, and so in the center of the square stone base was placed a little bit of a spire resembling a candle snuffer.

Immediately behind us was the woman we called the prima donna, who was always screeching hymns in my ear. In my youthful rudeness I used to turn around and scowl, hoping to stop her, but it seemed to have no effect. Mrs. McCumber, who sat in the same pew

The prima donna

with the prima donna, was a very fine woman. She always had a few words of greeting with us. Her face was somewhat masculine, her chin decidedly prominent. She usually wore a black silk dress and always drove a grey horse with her phaeton, which had a large umbrella top. Her aged father, a bewhiskered farmer, often accompanied her to church.

In the pew across the aisle and to the right of ours was Mr. Reardon, a hardware man, and his brother, an undertaker and furniture dealer. They both had grayish brown side whiskers and rather prominent chins, brown eyes and bald heads.

Sitting in the pew above Wing's was old man Jones, editor of the New York Times, and his family. They were summer residents. His coachman, in livery, always had a copy of his publication ready to hand him when he emerged from church. He would snatch it away from the coachman, get in his carriage, and glance at the headings.

Mr. Jones of the N.Y. Times

The minister was tall and slim, about fifty years of age. His sermons were rather long, but very good. During one, a big, fat perspiring colored woman came out of the vestry room, fanning herself with a palm leaf fan. She had on a white dress and a big straw hat with a grass wreath on it. She was back of the chancel rail when the minister turned and saw her. He then led her by the elbow through the gate of the rail and directed her to go up the aisle.

Instead of going up the aisle, however, she sat down on the steps of the chancel. She seemed overwhelmed with joy to think that she was sitting up there in front of the whole congregation. We found out later the poor woman was a half-wit.

Coming home from church on the Dutchess Turnpike we would generally see old Dr. Thorn driving his buckboard down Thorn Hill. He was so large and heavy that his buckboard bent low to the ground. He was too fat for his hands to reach the ordinary position of a driver, so he had to drive with his hands almost parallel to his hips. He was considered a good doctor of the old type. There was a community called Mechanic on the Dutchess Turnpike. It consisted of the Nine Partners boarding school, the Hicksite and Orthodox Quaker meeting houses, and an old inn. The inn had a store at one end and a ballroom typical of wayside inns of those days, with an arched ceiling, and there was a balcony for musicians.

Mechanic on the turnpike

All these buildings were of hewn timbers and weather boards, except the Orthodox Quaker Meeting House, which was built of bricks, with hewn timbers for the rafters and other roof timbers, and with four posts. The meeting house windows were nearly square and flaring toward the interior, with deep window sills. The outside doors were of plain wide boards with heavy wrought hinges reaching nearly across the door. Inside was the usual box stove and wooden benches with two straight wooden bars for backs. The roof was of wooden shingles, with little projection to the eaves and gable ends.

This meeting house was built under the supervision of my great grandfather, as was the Quaker boarding school, called Nine Partners.

I once attended a funeral at the Hicksite Meeting House which was built of hewn timbers and weather boarding. The minister, Dominie Pierce, who was not a Quaker, used as his text, "If thy father and mother forsake thee, the Lord will take thee up." We children, hearing this text, were much surprised to think that Milton Coffin, over whom the funeral services were being held, must have been deserted by his father and mother. They all seemed to be such good people.

Hicksites

We decided it must have been because he had married the widow Russel, yet we had never heard anything against her. Finally we decided that it was Dominie Pierce's fault, that he had misspoken himself in the text.

The land around the two meeting houses had originally belonged to the Orthodox Society, which of course included the cemetery. When the Society split, the land was equally divided, including the cemetery. The dividing fence between the two meeting houses was of boards running horizontally, about four feet high, cutting through the cemetery and leaving comparatively few graves in the Hicksite yard—all of whom had been Orthodox to begin with.

The divided Quakers

The same kind of division happened to a Quaker meeting house plot on a place called Quaker Hill about twenty miles from Mechanic. In later years the old fence was replaced by one of barbed wire, and General Lew Wallace (or perhaps it was my father) commented that the spirits of the two factions would catch on the barbs.

In the original Mechanic cemetery the gravestones were common slate fieldstones with the initials cut on them. As the Society of Quakers acquired more land and enlarged the cemetery, the graves began to be marked with more modern headstones.

Across the road from the meeting houses, up the hill a little, and to the left of the highway, stood the house of Mr. and Mrs. Congdon, good old interesting Quakers.

They had one of the sweetest gardens imaginable, which was below the gray stone wall on the west side of the house. I can especially remember the beautiful dark red Jacquemont roses. John Britton, colored, had been the gardener there for years, and took the greatest pride in showing people through the garden.

Further down the road toward Four Corners was the home of Deborah Willits, an old Quaker lady, exceedingly bright and interesting. Mrs. Willits could relate stories of many of her ancestors. She lived in a house with a small yard between it and the road, with a high horse block built in the picket fence near the gate. On the gate was a chain attached to a post in the yard, with a weight in the center to hold the gate shut. A short straight path led up to the porch, which was of Colonial design, with two round columns.

The entablature, with an elliptical arch, was covered with a shingled roof. The door had six vertical panels, a brass knocker, and a heavy handmade lock on the inside. This lock had an immense key. Above the transom bar was a fan light. Inside, the house was plain, with good San Domingo mahogany furniture.

Deborah Willits was always glad to see my father and to talk with him on historical and genealogical subjects. We all thought she was lovely. We were sure to come away with a basket of fruit from the trees in the rear of her house, especially when the large Bartlett pears were in season.

A lady's peaceful home

Most of our visits to her were on the way home from church on Sundays. Coming into Deborah's peaceful home was always such a relief to me after listening to the prima donna screeching hymns in the pew behind us.

On Tuesdays, market day, the Dutchess Turnpike would be lined with teams going to Poughkeepsie, eighteen miles west from Chestnut Ridge.

Many sloops plied the Hudson River, picking up and unloading freight at Poughkeepsie. Those wagons traveling westward on the turnpike often carried cargoes destined to become freight on the sloops. Coming eastward were empty wagons and fish-peddler carts.

When I was a boy, it was still common to see wagons that had long hubs made of locust, a very old type of hub. There were no springs under these wagons, which were noted for the tough, flexible iron used on them. This iron was made from charcoal iron and was said to have been pounded by hand from the cast pigs. For a seat was a "wagon chair," just like any old-fashioned, straight-backed chair, but extending across the body of the wagon and seating two people. In cold weather it was often covered with a buffalo robe.

I recall one of these old wagons passing us on a dusty fall day, a chair seat in front with two riders, and another behind with two more. The deep body of the wagon was imbedded with rice straw and filled with farm produce. One of the persons in the rear chair was an elderly lady with a white, haggard face and streaming gray hair. She leaned over the arm of the chair and had an absolutely blank expression. She was secured to the chair with a heavy black strap to keep from falling out. We assumed she was being taken to the asylum in Poughkeepsie. The other three persons with her seemed to be paying no attention to her as we watched the wagon disappear in the dust.

On the road to Pleasant Valley

One of the sights in Pleasant Valley was a three-wheeled wagon, the only one I've ever seen in my life. Two wheels were behind, with a sort of phaeton body, and the driver's seat was up over the one wheel in front. Beside this wagon was an old stagecoach, which was doubly interesting to me from having read and heard about stagecoach days. In school, our English primers showed stagecoaching along the green fields of England.

Like all stagecoaches of its day, this one hung on heavy leather straps, which preceded the use of springs. The paint was almost gone from the coach, but it had yellow wheels and a red body. Why this old open shed gave space to these two vehicles I never knew. The shed's roof was moss-covered and falling in from age.

The heads and hats of the drivers of wagons on market days on the turnpike were a mixed lot. The women mostly wore little, round straw bonnets. The men's hats ranged from broad-brimmed straw hats to stovepipe hats. The majority of the men's hats shaded whiskers.

Some of the farmers living at a distance would be up as early as two o'clock in the morning on market day to finish their milking, load the wagons, feed and water their horses, get their own breakfasts, and be underway before the heat of the sun began.

The loads in the wagons usually included bob calves, tied with their feet together, a front and hind foot crossed, tied as tightly as possible, making the calves bleat with pain during the journey. If you took calves loose in a crate to market it made the market men angry because it was not as convenient to weigh the calves on the stillyards. The market men hung them up by the rope around their feet, hooked them right on like dead things. Tied calves were often left lying in the broiling sun, panting.

Also loaded in the wagons were lambs, tied by the feet in the same way as the calves; and there were crates of chickens, packed so full that the feathers pressed out through the slats, causing dull mutterings and occasional prolonged squawks. These chicken crates were wedged in the wagons with bags of potatoes and barrels of apples. Some of the horses pulling the produce wagons had been discarded from the streetcars of New York City and sold through dealers to unscrupulous farmers. These were the days before enforcement by the Society for the Prevention of Cruelty to Animals.

Wagon loads and teams

"The Katzenbergs from Montgomery Place,"
by Benson Lossing.

Chapter XII
WORKMEN AT THE RIDGE

One year, Joe Titus the painter was working more or less all summer on our house. Joe was tall and skinny, with an enormous Adam's apple. He had light-colored, dead-looking hair and washed-out blue eyes. His white duck suit hung on him and flapped in the wind.

Joe seemed to delight in playing mean tricks on me. Once he asked me to smell a big, round brush full of green paint. I started to take a good smell of it when suddenly he shoved the brush and smeared paint all over my nose.

Joe Titus and his tricks

Another time I was raking the leaves off the garden path, working under a window and using a rake I had taken a lot of time to make. I had nailed two sticks together into a "T," driving nails through the crosspiece

137

for teeth. The painter suddenly leaned out the window and said, "Let's see your rake." I gave it to him and he broke the handle off and threw the rest back to me. Then he stirred his paint with the piece he kept.

In spite of Joe's mean tricks and sarcastic grin, I was fascinated with him and decided to be a painter, too. He used to let me paint a little once in a while. One day he was mixing paint at the east side of the house and he had left one pot nearly filled with gray paint standing on the lawn. Colored Gertrude and I thought it would be fun to run and jump over it.

This we did successfully several times, but I eventually landed in it and upset it. I still remember Joe holding my foot and scraping the paint off it back into the pot. The paint that fell on the grass left its mark there for years and years.

Mr. Butts hangs paper

Mr. Butts was the paperhanger who used to come out from Poughkeepsie. He was tall, with a long head, and had only one eye. I was afraid of him on account of his empty eye socket. Once when I smelled the glue melting for his paste I at first thought it was that terrible empty eye smelling.

Mr. Butts was a lordly sort of gentleman and didn't want young ones anywhere near him—ever. When he started papering around the arched windows in the library, he said it was a very difficult and particular job, so he shut the door and locked himself in. We suspected it was an excuse to loaf.

Mr. Lyons, the white-washer

Mr. Lyons, colored, also from Poughkeepsie, used to come to do our whitewashing. He was short and fat and his feet looked like duck bills. He was covered with pockmarks, the first I had ever seen, and a mystery to me and my younger sister. After smallpox was explained to me, I was afraid to go near him.

About this time, my sister was asking me a great

many questions as to what things were, how they were made, what they were for—and she always thought my explanations were wonderful. I felt the responsibility of explaining everything to her, whether I knew the real answer or not.

After Mr. Lyons left, she asked me how people got smallpox. I went to an old writing desk that opened like a box and opened it, telling her that when people put their heads over an open box like that, their faces would break out and it would be "small box." From then on we were very careful to avoid putting our heads over it.

John Williams was our plumber, a tall, knock-kneed Englishman with kind brown eyes. Mr. Williams was really a tinsmith by trade and he kept a tin store down in the village.

The plumber, a tall Englishman

Since he could solder a lead pipe, people called him in to do plumbing. He would tin a roof or solder a leak or mend a tea kettle. He also sold stoves and set them up, and he mended pumps. Everything he did was done perfectly.

One day, while he was trying to solder a little tin gun for me, I inquired about his wife, who had been ailing for a long time with heart trouble. He said, "Well, she's just like an old pump; her valves are worn out."

Eugene Bradford used to drive Mr. Williams up from Dover to The Ridge. Mr. Williams would sing hymns in his deep bass voice all the way up, the same hymns he sang in the choir at the Baptist Church on Sundays. If Mr. Williams was out of his shop, he left little Mr. Ambrose in charge. Mr. Ambrose had a cobbler's bench in one corner of the tin shop, and when a customer came in he had to stop his cobbling. Because he was nearsighted and had one short leg, he would look down at where he was going to step, then immediately look up to see where he was going. He continuously kept up that movement, saying to himself all the time, "I don't know where John keeps these things, or what he asks for them," and "John ought to be here, John ought to be here! Take what you want, take what you want! Pay for it when you come down again, pay for it when you come down again!"

Jim Russel worked for our farm and lived in the tenant house with his wife and ten-year-old son. Eventually, he built an extra room, and his doleful father and mother, Mr. and Mrs. Elijah Russel, also moved in.

Jim was a very large man, with broad shoulders and a large head, and his nose was rather hooked. His eyes were light blue, his whiskers long and light brown. His hands and feet were small, in fact his ankles were too small to support his weight, and he often turned them. Jim's expression was kindly, his voice loud and cheery. When at work he wore brown overalls and used to stand with his thumbs under his armpits.

Jim was an excellent farmer, early to rise, and finished his work by early evening. We children liked him, for he always had a pleasant word to say and would let us play in the hay and ride on loads of hay. He would let us do anything with the hay except slide down the haystacks.

In the early morning hours, when they were cooling the milk in forty-quart cans in the meadow spring, Jim would dip the long-handled quart measure in the can, fill it full, then stand there and laugh to see me drink it with my eyes bulging over the dipper.

Jim Russel admires my strength

Only one thing pleased him more, and that was to try my strength. He would show the different men how I could lift the end of an oxcart tongue, waist high. We used to go to his house for butter and eggs. Mrs. Russel opened the door and left it open while she went to get the eggs. Pompeii, their shepherd dog, would come out to greet us, and the canary birds in the house kept up a lively song. Jim's son, Walter, joined us in our home school, conducted by my mother. Walter was bright and always full of fun. He had some regular duties about the farm, such as hunting eggs, and we enjoyed going with him to the hay mows and to the nests in old wagons, under straw stacks and spruce trees and horse mangers as well as to the chicken house.

Another duty of Walter's was to drive the cows back and forth from the pasture, changing every week or so to different pastures. Pompeii was his constant companion. One night several sheep were killed in the neighborhood. Fearing Pompeii would be suspected, Walter picked the dog's teeth to make sure no wool was found in them. As the years went by, Jim Russel became interested in local politics and was elected pathmaster for the district from O'Brien's hill across to the other side of the second bridge at Bat O'Hearn's, and from our house to the boundary line of Jed Langdon's, a distance of three miles. A pathmaster's duties were to call the neighbors out to work on the road. Each neighbor was assessed according to the size of his farm and was required to work a certain number of days on the road—or he could pay a dollar a day to the town so a substitute could be hired.

Picking Pompeii's teeth

We were assessed twenty-one days. Providing a man counted as one day, but a team and a man counted four days. We usually worked our time out in about four days. Part could be done in the spring, part in the fall.

Becoming the pathmaster was the start of Jim's political career, but it marked the end of seven years of working on our farm. Very soon Mr. Stearns, the wagonmaker, was employed by Jim to make a new buckboard. If you saw a cloud of dust in the distance you knew it was Jim driving his new team and buckboard, electioneering.

Jim becomes pathmaster

Overalls became a thing of the past for him. His long brown hair was trimmed, and he became a hail fellow well met with everybody, the right-hand-man for the congressman in that locality. Jim later ran for superintendent of the poor and was elected. When that happened, he left a man in his place to finish the last year of work at The Ridge. He moved with his family into the superintendent's quarters at the County House, where he stayed through a second term.

Jim grew fatter, and could no longer put his thumbs under his armpits—he now clasped them across his stomach. As time went on he became severely criticized, and eventually retired from politics and bought a good farm in the town of Beekman.

Jerry Waldron, a carpenter who worked for my father, was also the village undertaker. Tall and skinny, with thin yellow whiskers, sharp features and very round shoulders, he had deep-set, keen blue eyes, with a troubled expression. He wore gray trousers, a brown cardigan jacket and a black slouch hat, and always carried a pencil over his right ear.

Mr. Waldron, carpenter, undertaker

Whenever Mr. Waldron sawed through a long board he would stop, hollow his chest, and give a deep, drawn-out cough. People said he had consumption. Whatever that was, I then wished I had it, too, for I loved Jerry Waldron and always imitated his cough when I sawed a board. Mr. Waldron smelled of tobacco, pine lumber and whiskey "for the consumption." He always smiled when he watched me trying to learn to use tools. One time when I was about ten years old, he and two or three men came to shingle the kitchen roof. I straightaway walked up the ladder with a bunch of shingles on my back and started shingling, too. When he saw me putting my nails right out in plain sight, he said in his feeble, drawling voice, "You must get right down off this roof as your father will only blame me if it leaks."

I moved and went over to the other side of a dormer

window, where he soon found me shingling again. He smiled and said, "Well, I will show you how to shingle." then taught me what he called the "three laps," keeping the nails under each lap. He let me help until the roof was finished.

Mr. Talliday always came to work with him. Quite an old man, Mr. Talliday had short-cropped gray whiskers and a dried-up complexion, his spectacles the most prominent thing about his face. His work clothes were similar to Mr. Waldron's.

Waldron and Talliday argue

The pair of them were always arguing, Mr. Waldron in his feeble drawl, Mr. Talliday seeming to draw words in instead of letting them out. Mr. Waldron would insist that a door should be two feet six inches wide, and Mr. Talliday would insist it should be two feet four. They would both keep on working and arguing.

Mr. Waldron would lose his temper and hitch his long body around, but Mr. Talliday's little, short figure never showed any agitation. Instead, he would make some droll remark about Mr. Waldron's undertaking business, such as "almost time to box up old Mrs. Hogan." Mr. Waldron would give a sickly smile, and they would be all ready for the next argument.

My sister must have been a trial to Mr. Waldron, as she would get right under his heels. Once when he was ripping a board we held flower pot saucers under the end of the saw to catch the sawdust for our play gardens. He glared at us and drawled, "You young ones must keep out of my way!"

Another time they were putting a small addition on one corner of the house and we got up on the scaffold to see what he had been doing, when he came up with a board in his hand. We ran around to the other side and to the corner, as far as we could go, only to find it was the spot he was headed for. So we jumped down the seven feet into mud.

Mr. Waldron came to work driving a gray horse, one

143

of the two that he also drove with the hearse. He would be carrying his dinner pail as he walked up to the house, the tin cup turned upside down on the top of the pail. He had to hold his forefinger on the cup to keep it from falling off. This dinner pail was made in the Williams Tin Shop, a very inexpensive thing. My mother humored me and got me one when my admiration for Mr. Waldron took the form of wanting a dinner pail just like his.

Whenever Mr. Waldron had a funeral at hand his spirits seemed to rise. His funeral parlor consisted of a room in the back of the carpenter shop. When he conducted a funeral he wore a Prince Albert coat, white gloves, and a stovepipe hat, and he was all smiles. In fact, he was the gayest undertaker I have ever seen.

Mr. Talliday drove the hearse while Mr. Waldron sat beside him. The hearse was painted a dull flat black and had seen its best days. It had crinkly yellow-gray silk curtains and a row of black, wooden plumes all around the top. The last time I saw Mr. Waldron was years after he had moved away from the village. We happened to meet in a blacksmith's shop. He was very feeble and smelled strongly of whiskey.

Waldron, Talliday and the hearse

Lon Townsend was a genuine "botch carpenter." He built a porch on our home and instead of having the gutter run away from the house it ran toward the house. To rectify this mistake he cut a pier off under the floor and let the porch down on that corner. He seemed wonderfully proud of the achievement, regardless of the floor being low on that corner.

A botch carpenter

Mr. Townsend was tall, with a big droopy mouth and moustache, a high nose, sleepy blue eyes and thick black hair always matted with hair oil that you could smell all over the house—even sometimes drowning out the smell of his whiskey. He was always cross.

Once he put a set of double doors between our dining room and parlor. The doors had eleven mistakes on them. In the first place he cut the rough opening two inches too big, so after he left one day I decided I would plaster up around it. In my childish ignorance I got together some lath, lime and coarse gravel then found that I had no hair to mix with the mortar. I happened to notice that Hawkeye was shedding, so I got my sister's comb and combed the poor dog until he began to whimper and stagger about. After a fashion I covered up mistake number one of Mr. Townsend's.

Doors with eleven mistakes

One of the doors he fitted upside down. Another door he cut too short and was nailing a piece on the bottom when my father spoke to him about it. Mr. Townsend replied "Jerry Waldron always puts pieces on the bottom of his doors."

My father refused to be convinced. Then Mr. Townsend pulled out a ten-dollar bill from his vest pocket and threw it down on the saw horse, saying, "Send and get new doors." My father said, "Have you had your dinner yet, Mr. Townsend?"

Townsend sheepishly picked up the ten dollars and returned it to his pocket.

That particular set of doors has always been a monument to his trade. Every once in a while we used to go through the ceremony of pointing out the eleven mistakes to visitors.

An old soul named Pat O'Brien used to come up on Chestnut Ridge and do a day's work for the different farmers. He was tall, large-boned, and had a nice Irish face, with heavy dark eyebrows over blue eyes, somewhat faded from his seventy years.

Pat O'Brien dies alone in winter

Pat went from house to house, working, whenever the weather was fit, and I imagine he spent the cold winters at the County House, as many of these old fellows did. One spring morning on Hustead's hill, where the road had been very deep with drifts for weeks, a piece of black cloth showed above the melting snow. No one thought anything of it for several days, but finally enough snow melted away so it showed the black hat and part of the face of Pat O'Brien.

The coroner was summoned, and the body was dug out of the snow. Someone hung O'Brien's hat on the rail fence, and it continued to hang there for months.

The first I saw of Jack Kearney, he came with a gang of seventeen men to work on a rock cut for basements of some buildings for the Brothers of Nazareth. These workmen came from the Clove iron ore mines.

Jack was an old sailor from the crew of the sailing ship Dreadnaught, commanded by the famous Captain Samuels. Jack was in the navy during the Civil War, on the Wabash. He was still immensely strong, though probably about sixty. When excavating these cellars he struck drill with Maurice Whalen, as most of the rock drilling was done by hand in those days. He also fired the shots.

Irish brawlers

Jack was thickset and smooth-shaven, with large features and keen blue eyes. He wore blue overalls with a belt, a red flannel shirt and blue jumper, which set off his short, iron-gray hair. He always talked with his teeth set together, and weighed each word well before he spoke it. He was forever in a fight, but oddly enough always seemed to be in the right. I remember one fight with Martin Gallagher, who with Joe Gilmore was drilling a hole close to Jack's.

Gallagher made the remark that Jack didn't strike hard enough to crack a walnut. He no sooner got the remark out of his mouth than Jack had him on the ground, choking him. As he grabbed, Jack cut Gallagher's chin with his thumbnail, and with a choking voice, Gallagher begged, "Don't tear my jacket!"

Mike Joyce was another old Irishman, so intemperate

that he was palsied, but in spite of it he was an excellent hand to cradle grain.

Mike would cradle all day long in the hot sun and no one could cut him out of his swath, even though he was old and half drunk. He was short and wiry, with a pinched red face, all eaten up with drink. He always talked to himself. Even if you were talking to someone else, old Mike sometimes would come up and keep stepping one foot to the other, muttering to himself.

Mike Joyce cradles grain

*"The Battery and Castle Garden," by Benson Lossing
in the mid-19th century.*

Chapter XIII
OUR IMMIGRANT FARMHANDS

It came to pass that farm labor was scarce. Many workers who once had been available bought farms of their
own. This made it necessary for us and others to get
hired help from a greater distance.

Farmers began importing their help from Castle Garden, the New York immigrant station situated in the
building which later became the Aquarium at Battery
Park. To hire help, Mother would leave for New York
on the 9:15 morning train and stay with Jennie and
Cornelia Donnelon, who lived in a handsome old
brownstone-front house at 16 Pacific Street, Brooklyn.

At the time it was built, this house was in what was
considered one of the best residential sections. The

*Mother
goes to
Castle
Garden
for new
help*

Donnelons had lived on the farm next to us for a while, and a warm friendship had been formed. After the night's stay at the Donnelons, Mother would take Jennie with her to Castle Garden to help pick out the man.

These recently landed immigrants were called "greenhorns," and lived up to the name. We never knew the basis of Mother's selection of help.

Immigrant
workers
come
and go

Harry, a young Russian Jew was the first. Evidently he had never done any physical work in his life. He had a very mild, smiling face, big dark brown sleepy eyes, bushy black hair, no beard. At the start, Harry kept scratching his head. As soon as Mother turned him over to me (though I was only eleven) I took him out to a clump of evergreens. There I cut his hair, which was literally crawling, then made him take off his clothes and scrub.

Harry stayed a month, digging a pond, and was so worthless as a worker that we had to let him go. Mother soon went back to New York for another helper.

Herman Mueller, a German, was next. Short and thickset, with blue eyes, yellow hair and a florid complexion, Herman was exceedingly clean and had a military bearing. He was a good worker, but was always angry about something. Once, when he started to lift a chicken coop, a board came off, flew up and hit him on the nose. He immediately smashed the coop to pieces.

Another time we happened to have salt mackerel for breakfast, and all that morning Herman hoed corn at a terrific rate. I finally ventured to ask him what was the matter.

He swore a mighty German oath, then said, "Geben Fleisch!" He wanted us to give him meat, not salt mackerel.

Herman was forever quoting Bismarck. Only once did he let down from his military attitude. That was on a trip to town when he told me a story about a German empress who wanted a sleigh ride when there was no snow. All the loyal peasants spread salt on the road for miles and miles and gave the empress her wish.

As the season advanced and more work came on, another pilgrimage was made to New York and Mother brought back Joseph, a Swiss. He was tall, strong, with a free, happy air, was a good cowherd and a wonderful yodeler.

Yodeling Swiss cowherds and German peasants

At first he had seemed delighted to get up early and work in the fields, and undoubtedly would have remained in contentment had not Herman bred discontent in him. Joseph left before the end of his first month. As soon as Herman got rid of Joseph, he left himself.

Another trip to New York, and Mother brought back Rudolph, his wife, Marry, and their two-year-old child, Anna. Rudolph was a tall, blue-eyed German with white hands. He had an air of superiority toward his wife and toward our family in general. He brought a large accordion with him, which he played on a summer's evening while sitting on the kitchen porch.

Marry was more of a peasant type, rather short and round-shouldered, with broad hips and masculine features. She wore "slips" on her feet instead of shoes. Her voice was harsh, and she wheezed when she talked. Even her smile was hard. She was very strong and a good worker.

Little Anna had curly yellow hair and blue eyes. As soon as she cried, her father or mother quickly stood her on her head. She seemed to like this rough treatment and would stop crying immediately.

Through the day, Anna received no attention from her father or mother, and could be seen sitting out with the chickens, watching them, or playing with an assortment of old cans. She would look up and smile through the dirt on her face. She couldn't speak a word, but had a grunting language of her own. When Rudolph was playing his accordion in the evening, Marry would knit big, thick blue socks like those she wore in her slips. As he played, Rudolph would say, "Dance, Anna, dance!" Without lifting her feet from the ground, Anna would turn round and round, always bringing her left heel to the center of her right foot.

Rudolph broke almost everything he touched, but if reproved he would say, "I break all, I fix all." He was never known to fix anything and was absolutely useless. He was supposed to be the gardener and, under direction, had planted quite a large garden. When the lima beans came up and the split bean showed in the little shoot above the ground, he pulled each one up and replanted it, root up and bean in the ground. This was greatly amusing to me and to Eugene Bradford.

Eugene did something one day to annoy Marry, and she chased him out of the house, hitting him across the mouth with a beefsteak. Another time, as I was coming up the stone step in front of the kitchen porch, Marry was coming out of the house with a pan of dishwater in her hands and slipped on a potato skin. Down she went with the dishpan, her feet up in the air and her slips flying off. I couldn't help but laugh. She rolled over, got up as quick as a flash and hit me in the face with the dish rag.

Getting even with Marry

Late that afternoon, Marry finished her work, closed the blinds in the kitchen, and kicked off her slips, leaving them beside the kitchen door while she went upstairs for a nap. Anna was left entertaining herself on the kitchen porch near a pail of water that stood there.

The slap with the dishrag had left me with a mental sting, so I pointed out the slips to Anna. She picked them up and grunted. I grunted and pointed to the water pail. She grunted and I grunted. Then she dropped the slips in the water, where I presume Marry found them when she came downstairs.

This family stayed with us about three months.

So Mother went to Castle Garden again and this time

brought back Mattias and Mary. Mattias was Swiss and his wife was German. It must have been after dusk when Mother picked out Mattias, for he looked like an anarchist from head to foot. He had such a fiery red face and his whiskers bushed out like a scared woodchuck's. He had snappy, wild eyes and carried a revolver and dirk knife and chattered incessantly.

Again to Castle Garden

Eugene and I decided we had to get that revolver away from Mattias, so Eugene got an old army musket and traded with him. The musket was so long and unwieldy that we felt safer.

Mary looked exactly like Marry, and was angry all the time. She particularly hated Eugene. They only stayed until their month was out, then left in a terrible huff. Evidently they packed the stock of the old musket in their belongings, but the end of the long barrel showed below Mary's heavy black skirts. How she ever managed to sit down with it I don't know.

The day after they returned to New York my father got a letter from them saying they had liked the place very much but had suffered much from our "he, black servant."

Mother then went to the St. Gotthard Hotel in New York, where there was an employment agency run by Mr. and Mrs. Nedderman, a Swiss couple who had a little son, Igene.

This time Mother drew John Sheis, his wife, Lena, and a friend named Elise, all of them being relatives of the Nedderman's, just arrived from Switzerland. These people were fine in every way. John was a diligent, good worker on the farm, besides being a good harness-maker. Lena was the cook and Elise the upstairs girl.

John Scheis

They stayed a year or so, went back to Switzerland for a visit, and then wrote asking to come back, but we could not make a place for them.

John had woodwork going every evening. He made little Swiss-style houses and small and large bird cages of thin material that he used to send for from New York. He sold these items in New York, one bird cage going for as much as nineteen dollars. By comparison, John's wages were twelve dollars a month, Lena's and Elise's ten dollars each.

When we took this particular bird cage in a sleigh to the depot, I sat with it on my lap, atop a load of hay. John drove the team as I held onto the cage. The roads were very icy and, as we rounded a curve, the sleigh slid off into the ditch and upset. The top of the load slid off, I with it, but right side up, still holding the bird cage, which was undamaged. We reloaded, and drove on to the depot.

In the summer months, when John and Lena were still with us, the Neddermans came up to visit them and brought Flora, their beagle hound. The visit lasted two weeks. Igene had never been on a farm before, and he and Flora had a grand time. Flora was so happy on the farm that they left her with us until John and Lena departed months later.

Early in November, John fitted himself out with new rubber boots, a pair of Arctics, and evening slippers.

Burned slippers

The latter two pair he kept in the oven of the old range that was bricked into the kitchen fireplace. When Thanksgiving arrived a fire was lit in the old stove, and as a queer odor filled the kitchen, poor John suddenly remembered his footware.

He hurriedly opened the oven door, and the smoke rolled into the room. As he pulled out his charred Arctics and slippers he said, "Jimminy pelch!" and looked very sad.

Lizzie, the upstairs girl

Later, Mother brought back Lizzie, an Englishwoman, to do the cooking and upstairs work. Mother also brought an English man to work on the farm. The man turned out to be useless. After he left, we got a letter from Ludlow Street jail in New York. He wanted us to come down and get him out.

Lizzie was short, rather thickset, and had a long black braid hanging down her back. She always had a nauseated expression. She had worked in the English potteries and knew nothing about housework. The months she stayed with us became known as the "Lizzie Summer," because she was often claiming to be sick and my sisters waited on her all the time, even cooking breakfast and taking it up to her.

Old Sarah Riley was a big-boned, broad-hipped, short Irish cook. We lost track of how many times she asked off to go to her brother's funeral.

Returning intoxicated from one of these trips, Sarah described to my younger sister how her brother had died. While she was telling it, she could hardly stand still and rolled her eyes so. She had a few pieces of money tied up in her pocket handkerchief and kept twisting it all the time she talked. I suddenly asked her if she ever played "Catch Wild Geese." She asked how, and I told her to do as I told her.

I pulled two pieces of long, dry, red-topped grass and told her to open her mouth. Then I laid the grass through her mouth like a horse's bit, and with the grass crossed told her to shut her mouth. Then I drew the grass through her teeth and she began spitting out the hayseed. She was too drunk to be angry, and I was too young to be ashamed of my trick.

Teasing Sarah Riley

Father brought Charles Wester, a Swiss, from Castle Garden to be a farmhand, and he stayed with us from summer through part of the winter. Charles was an excellent worker, a good mechanic and a wood-turner by trade. He was a handsome man, tall and well-built and immensely strong, with dark hair and moustache. The tip of his nose had been split by a knife.

At first, Charles and I got along well. He showed me

how to do many mechanical things, such as make Swiss puzzle boxes, ox bows and ax handles. On New Year's Day, with the weather bright and frost out of the top of the ground, Charles and I took my uncle's horses (being boarded with us for winter) and rode them bareback over The Ridge into Clove Hollow. We returned by way of Jackie Duncan's, over Stearn's Road and through the woods, a delightful ride of six miles.

We were interested in everything we came to—the people, the houses, and the way the road wound down into Clove Hollow. This was my first trip there, and I thought the old-time stores and Colonial houses very beautiful in their setting. After that trip, our family took frequent drives to Clove Hollow, a warm, sheltered spot where crops matured two weeks earlier than on The Ridge.

We later found out Charles had a terrible temper at times. He seemed to have a mania for collecting guns, owning two or three rifles and a couple of revolvers. My mother finally told him he must get rid of some of his guns, that she could not have them lying around in the kitchen or on the stoop. His face turned red and sullen, his black eyes flashed, and he flew into a rage. He took two or three of the guns out on the chopping block, split the stocks all up with the axe, flattened the barrels and bent them double.

A bad Swiss temper

Then he came into the house and demanded his money, threatening to pound my father, and calling my mother names. He went out again and started to come back in, but I locked the door against him. He came around the house and burst in the front door, but by that time I had a .32 revolver and sat quietly at the head of the dining room table, the revolver under the tablecloth. I watched him swinging his arms at my father. I was ready to shoot Charles if he hit him. My mother already had gone for Oliver Lawrence, a neighbor.

My father succeeded in quieting Charles, who collected his pay and left. Mr. Lawrence got there too late for the excitement. Charles had no doubt been under the influence of hard cider that he got from one of our neighbors. When he was himself he was a very good, willing man. A year or two afterwards, he wanted to work for us again, but we did not take him back.

*Charles
leaves
in anger*

"Surf Bathing Near the Pavilion, Coney Island,"
by Benson Lossing.

Chapter XIV
VISITING NEW YORK CITY

The train from Dover to New York had open platform cars, no air brakes—the braking all being done by hand—and the tops of the smokestacks were fitted with spark arrestors for burning wood, though by this time they were burning coal.

To the city by train

The engine was twenty-five ton. The cars were fitted with four wheeltrucks and lit inside by kerosene lamps. They were upholstered with red plush, and in place of shades that pulled up and down they had wooden blinds. Many of the cars were trimmed with black walnut and bird's-eye maple.

On train trips to New York my Mother carried a black satchel made of soft leather to hold our train lunch. I was allowed to go down the aisle pretending to sell tickets, a game which passengers were willing to play with me. After these trips I would play train at home. From some place I had gotten an old railroad lantern marked "New York Central." It had a plain glass globe and I used to wrap a red cravat around it to make a red light.

I would carry it on my arm, a basket on the other arm, and go down to the cellar after apples. I could hardly see because of the cravat over the light.

The first I remember about New York was coming up the stone steps from the depot and a lot of soldiers were ahead of us on the steps. It was a long walk through the train shed out to 42nd Street.

In the depot of the New York Central's Harlem Division, was a row of light blue plaster columns, a big brown earthen spittoon beside each one. The pedestals of these columns were fluted and painted alternately, brown and yellow, with a brown base. Seats were along the walls, and all had dividers of iron with brass lions' heads on them. At each end of the depot was a red marble niche in the wall with two nickel faucets and heavy flat dippers hanging by chains so that cold water might be drunk.

*The depot
of the
N.Y. Central*

Beside one of these niches was the familiar sight of colored Ann, in a white apron, at the service of lady travelers and children. Ann would sit and crochet and knit and smile, and she was known for years as "Ann at the Depot."

Once out on 42nd Street we were opposite the portal of the Fourth Avenue horsecar tunnel. There we went through a din of tobacco-chewing cab drivers all shouting, "Cab, cab! Want a cab?" They were dressed in dark blue livery with nickel buttons and stove pipe hats, and they carried whips. The city smelled of soft coal, and from then on the busy streets with their whiff of coal tar never failed to thrill me.

Horsecars

Horsecars stood beside the row of cabs, and above the din of the cab drivers could be heard the jingle of the bells on the harnesses of the horsecar horses. The jingle and the noise intensified as we rode through the Fourth Avenue tunnel. For light, this tunnel had many round openings at the top, surrounded by iron vents. The walls and arched roof were of brick, painted white. The tunnel extended from 42nd Street to 34th, where steps led to the street.

To the left of 42nd Street and Fourth Avenue stood the Grand Union Hotel. Many people from the country chose this as their hotel, but Mother more often took us to the Westminster Hotel on 16th Street. On one of the trips, when I was about eight years old, we stayed at Miss Van Reiper's boarding house on 34th Street, she and my mother being former school mates.

A 34th-St. boarding house

We stayed in this handsome boarding house for a week and had grand things to eat. The boarders sat at a long dining table, beautifully set with silver and cut glass. Miss Van Reiper, a tall, rather slender lady of about fifty, sat at the head of the table, dressed in black. She always gave stern orders to the Irish waitress.

On one occasion the gas was turned up too high in the chandelier overhead and began to flutter. The waitress was told to tend to it, and the inexperienced girl pulled out a chair, stepping from it onto the set table with her great big feet in front of us all. Then she turned down the gas.

Miss Van Reiper reared up like a horse and shouted, "Stupid!" The girl grinned and got out.

One of the boarders was a Mrs. Clapp, a lady of about sixty-five, rather masculine, and with gray curls. She would walk into the parlor every evening in a very stately manner, black skirts rustling, a chess board under her arm. Because there was no one else, she would invite me to play with her. Chess was my favorite game at home, as my little sister and I had learned

Mrs. Clapp challenges me to chess

to play from a book and we practiced constantly. I found it easy to outplay Mrs. Clapp, but whenever I did so, she would look at me in such an ugly way that I let her win most of the time. When I did beat her, she invariably wanted to change chairs before she would play the next game. As a gift, Mrs. Clapp gave me a checkerboard puzzle.

Across the street from Miss Van Reiper's, a church was being built, and from our room's window it was very interesting to see the stone cutters carving the Gothic arches. I would watch them for hours at a time, as well as observe other aspects of the construction.

I watch a church being built

Those were the days before suspended scaffolding, and the scaffold poles were tall spruce timbers set in barrels on the sidewalk, the barrels filled with earth to keep them from slipping on the pavement. The brackets the planks rested on were also spruce timbers that ran into the walls of the church, where a stone had been left out for the purpose. This was called a "put hole." The other end of the timber was lashed to the perpendicular pole with a half-inch rope, tied with a special knot.

There were no machines to crush stone for concrete, so it was all done by hand out in the street, where loads of stone would be dumped. Stone was broken with long-handled hammers, the face of the hammer being about the size of a fifty-cent piece. The laborers were Irish and smoked stubby clay pipes. The hod carriers wore blue overalls and red flannel shirts and a belt around their waists.

After the workmen left for the day, kids used to come along and pick up barrel staves for firewood.

On a trip to New York, Mother and I boarded a horsecar, and one of her gold cuff buttons fell off and rolled down into the gratings of the floor. As I was taught not to say too much in the presence of elders, I waited until we got off the car, back to the sidewalk, to tell her about it.

In those days beggars were allowed on the streets. I remember one big, fat woman sitting by an iron fence. She pulled up her dress and showed my mother an immense ankle, so my mother would pity her affliction. I happened to spy a hole in her stocking, which showed it had been stuffed with newspaper.

Once, we went to the aquarium, taking my younger sister with us. We saw an awesome dolphin swimming in the big glass tank with many other fish, which gave us topics of conversation for months.

A trip from Grand Central Terminal took us to Stewart's dry goods store, where Wanamaker's now stands. I remember it had three or four storys; the windows were arched and had dark blue shades. We could look out on Grace Church. I remember being in the store while my mother was picking out sashes for my little sister and me. Hers was blue silk with a suggestion of plaid in it, and mine was a plaid with some blue in it, a good deal of yellow and some red, with long yellow and white fringes on it. I loved this sash and loved to see my sister with hers on.

Sashes for sister and me

The Vienna Bakery next to Grace Church had the most delicious hot chocolate with whipped cream on top. We used to go there every time we visited New York. We would drink the chocolate and eat the Vienna rolls, and to my delight there never seemed to be any limit put on us.

Once, my mother went to Altman's to get a hat for my younger sister. As my sister was not with us at the time, Mother sat me on a stool and an endless succession of girls' hats were tried on me. Mother would back off and tilt her head from one side to the other and absentmindedly tell me to sit still. The clerks and cash girls were all laughing, but it was a horrible ordeal for me—I felt about an inch high.

Broadway
omnibuses

On Broadway, the main transportation consisted of big white omnibuses, each with a door in the rear connected by a strap to the driver's seat. The driver was on top in front so he could open and shut the door easily.

These omnibuses had very heavy wheels and were high and hard to get into. Seats ran along the side, and the whole body of the omnibus sloped to the rear. When it was loaded there was always a sensation of crush as the passengers all slipped toward the rear end.

In front was the cash box, high up, and the passengers had to walk up there to put in the fare. From a hole in the top, the driver could look down and see the amount of change deposited. Passengers pulled a bell rope when wishing to get off. Those who could not find a seat hung onto straps overhead.

Broadway was almost impossible to cross, and the sound of these omnibuses and the trucks rattling over cobblestones was terrific. On nearly every corner was a policeman dressed in blue uniform and helmet-shaped hat. My mother always took the opportunity for escort across Broadway.

Then there was the trip to Battery Park, with its green lawns and hundreds of sparrows hopping about. From there we took the glorious ferryboat ride to Staten Island for a nickel. I remember on one of these trips watching two bootblacks find a cigar butt in the scupper on deck. They lit it, and first one, then the other,

Battery
Park

would puff it. I quite envied them their free life. These bootblacks were in all parts of the city, running around with their little shine boxes that were used as a foot rest for customers, and hung by a strap around the shoulder when not in use.

Grant's body

I remember the death of President Grant in 1885. Grant's body lay in state at City Hall, and the steps were roped off, except for the entrance. When we got there, an immensely long line of people was at this entrance, causing our hopes of getting in to fade. Then my mother boldly walked up to a policeman and told him we had come a long way from the country and had to return by the afternoon train.

He raised the rope so we could go under and motioned us to follow. We walked for some distance through City Hall until we came to the casket where Grant lay. I remember his face and gray whiskers. His casket was covered with flowers.

In our Harper's Weekly I was much interested in pictures of the transport from Egypt of Cleopatra's Needle, the obelisk that now stands near the Metropolitan Museum.

Cleopatra's Needle is raised

Harper's description of the remodeling of ships' hatches and the method of lowering the obelisk into the holds was illustrated, and very fascinating to me. After Cleopatra's Needle arrived in New York, Mother took me to see it as it lay on its side. It was blocked up in a sloping position, heeled against its foundation, and the tackle was being prepared to raise it.

Upon a subsequent visit after it was raised, I was disappointed that Cleopatra's Needle did not look to be a mile high. It is of a rather soft sandstone covered with hieroglyphics badly worn away on two sides. I was especially interested in the bronze crabs on each corner upon which it stands.

At this time the New York World Building and the Field Building north of Battery Park were the tallest in the city. On 81st Street, between Madison Avenue and Central Park, there were only two brownstone-front houses, standing close together on the north side. On the south side and nearly opposite was a small wooden house. Otherwise there were only vacant lots. North of the Harlem River were scattered squatter's shacks with goats rummaging in old tomato cans. This condition extended for quite a distance south of the Harlem River toward 125th Street. The river itself was full of masts of schooners, sloops and smaller vessels.

It always gave me a thrill as our train crawled over the drawbridge across the Harlem River. After crossing, the trainmen would light the oil lamps hanging overhead in the aisle, preparatory to running into the Park Avenue Tunnel. They also would close every window and ventilator. After entering the tunnel with its pitchy darkness, it was exciting to smell the gas from the soft coal. I would press my nose to the window pane and cup my hands at my eyes to see trackmen standing at frequent intervals in niches in the side of the tunnel as the train whizzed by.

Railroad drawbridge and tunnels

The brakeman, coming and going through the train, would open and shut doors as quickly as possible, but even then a cloud of smoke entered the car. In passing the light and ventilator openings we would catch a glimpse of the brakemen standing on the platforms at the ends of the cars, gradually twisting brake wheels by hand, in response to the engineer's signals, sounded on the train's whistle.

The brakemen would lean out to listen for the next signal, red bandana handkerchiefs, worn around their necks to keep out cinders, streaming in the wind. A signal might cause them to turn quickly to their brakes and set them tight. Then at last they would gradually release the brakes as our train made a flying switch into the train shed, past our own engine.

The brakemen

The brakemen wore dark blue (usually faded to green) heavy woolen caps, which could be pulled tight down over their ears in cold weather. I remember them in winter getting off the freight trains at Dover with long icicles on their moustaches. They would come into the station room and thaw them out.

It was in New York, when I was ten years old, that I was treated by a celebrated surgeon for the broken arm I suffered when our horse Fannie backed with me.

An ordeal
at the
surgeon's

At home the old country doctor said my arm was not broken but that my shoulder was dislocated. He set me on the floor and took my coat and shirt off. With a man on one side of me, the doctor went to the other and put his foot under my arm, and they both pulled until they got the ball of the shoulder into place. Then they put it in a sling and bandaged the arm.

They bound all my fingers in, bandaging the arm tight from the tip of my fingers to the shoulder. Then the arm was soaked in laudanum and I was taken home. The arm was left like that for about a month, when the bandage was taken off and my arm remained in a sling.

Then my cousin Adele Titus and I were playing a game and she fell heavily against my arm. It began to pain me severely, and so the old doctor again was called for. He said he would bring another doctor and a machine for fixing it the next day. My mother decided instead to take me to a doctor in New York.

The next morning, she and my father brought me to the office of Dr. Marco, the most celebrated surgeon in New York. He called in consultation—his son and Dr. Sands. They examined my arm, worked it up and down, and found it had been broken as well as dislocated. Dr. Marco drew a picture of the bone so my parents could see it had knit with an offset.

Then they withdrew to another room and I heard them discussing the advisability of breaking and resetting my arm, with the strong possibility that it might be paralyzed in so doing. If not rebroken, however, it would always be a badly crippled arm.

The operation was decided upon, so we went immediately to the Westminster Hotel. There we had a large room fronting on 16th Street, with a bowed window in one corner looking out on Union Square. That evening, doctors Marco and Sands came, gave me ether and laid me down flat on the floor. Dr. Marco put his foot under my arm and rebroke it. The next thing I knew I heard someone say, "Give him some soda water to settle his stomach."

My operation on the floor

At first my arm was in a sling and held with broad adhesive tape, secured to my side and over my shoulders, halfway down my back. No splint was used. The arm remained in this position for six weeks, the first three weeks of which were spent in New York at the Westminster.

When we had left home the fields of early spring were brown, an occasional snowbank lying in the corners by rail fences. Now, the grass was beginning to get green in New York parks and the sparrows were busy hopping all over. As soon as my arm was better my mother and I took many a little trip to spots of interest about the city, with an occasional visit to Staten Island.

Seeing the sights while I recuperate

We would go over to Brooklyn, crossing on the Fulton Ferry at the foot of Fulton Street to give me the pleasure of the ferry trip. From the trains of the Third Avenue Elevated the masts of sailing ships could be seen at both the east and west waterfronts at the same time. The Brooklyn Bridge was not yet completed.

On one visit to New York my mother took me on a Belt Line horsecar, which consisted of a small streetcar painted white and green with the number large on the front. Car seats ran lengthwise and were covered with carpet; tiny coal stoves were in the corner. These cars were drawn by teams of horses with rope traces to the harness. The horses were mostly poor, skinny old beasts.

The driver wore no uniform, but instead had a patched overcoat. He carried a whip and worked the brakes by hand. The conductor had a little bell punch strapped around his waist to register the fares.

My mother took me on one of these horsecars to a

wharf on the East River, where I saw my first sailing ship up close. The riverfront was lined with bowsprits reaching over the cobblestones of the streets, working lazily up and down with the rise and fall of the water. Bales of cotton, barrels of molasses and other merchandise were piled high on the dock.

East River docks and ships

At noontime, all the horses along the wharf ate from their nosebags. The smell of the horses combined with that of the river and the salt air fascinated me as Mother and I crossed the street among the trucks and longshoremen. She went a short way out on the dock with me, then stopped because of her timidity. She let me go a little closer, though.

There was a Dutch ship, painted green, loading or discharging a cargo of rails. The men wore light blue sailor clothes. When I looked on that ship it seemed like paradise to me, just like the pictures in my primer. The same thrill of being in the presence of a ship has never left me. I've never gotten over the sight of masts and yardarms and the sound of ropes running over the pulley sheaves.

At the end of those three weeks we returned to The Ridge, and my arm soon healed. From that time on it was perfectly comfortable.

Study of a woman with parasol, by Benson Lossing.

Chapter XV
THE COUNTY FAIR

The Dutchess County Fair was held at Washington Hollow, a central location in the county, twelve miles from our place.

The road we took to the fair led first over a ridge, two miles from home, where we owned twenty-two acres of high meadow land. From this meadow we could see seven counties of three states: New York, Connecticut and the Berkshire hills of Massachusetts. On a clear day, if we looked toward the northwest (with Stissing Mountain on the right) over the Hudson valley, we could see the Mountain House in the Catskills fifty miles away. The eye could follow the Hudson River valley from the Catskills to the Storm King and West Point below.

The road to the fair

After leaving this ridge and passing the Jonathan Husted place and the long watering trough set at a convenient height for horses, we descended Husted's hill. About halfway down this hill was a little cemetery, doubly enclosed by a dense hedge of arbor vitae and a wall of fieldstone. One of the marble gravestones was inscribed:

A blooming youth, a faded flower
Cut down and withered within an hour.

At the foot of the hill was a small stream and beyond it what we termed the "old tavern," then in use as a farm house. This was the junction of the Dutchess Turnpike, near Mutton Hollow. A half mile further on we passed through a hamlet called Little Rest. A small white house was at the left of the road, and also a building that had been a blacksmith's shop.

Mutton Hollow, Little Rest, and other places

The house was occupied by an old, one-armed man, a bachelor brother of the Hoaglands. He invariably would be in the blacksmith's shop standing in front of the long window over the work bench, dressed in blue overalls and jumper, busied in chewing tobacco.

From Little Rest the road led over Thorne hill, down through Mechanic, then to the Four Corners, from which a road branched off left to the County House. The home and office of "Doc" Wardell was just at the entrance of Four Corners. The office window was decorated with a pasteboard rooster stuck to the pane.

Doc Wardell was tongue-tied and once when I consulted him about a bunch on the upper joint of our horse Bonnie's front leg, he said it was a "Who boil," caused by Bonnie lying with his foot doubled under him and pressing his iron shoe against the joint.

Across the road was the Dutch Reformed Church. A mile or so further on was the stock farm of Edwin Thorne, a breeder of fine trotting horses. After

Sharpsteen's hill came the toll gate with the keeper forever sticking his head out to see that he missed no one and the three-cent toll. Just beyond was a large watering tub, with a willow tree growing in the middle of it, and beyond that, a quarter of a mile, was Wheeler's Hotel, with stables across the road.

Wheeler's Hotel

This hotel stood in a corner of the fair grounds, its long piazza fronting the turnpike. Wheeler was a typical old inn host, a man of about sixty-five, short and thick-set, with a rugged, cleanshaven face. He always wore a dark suit, a stovepipe hat and stiff white collars and cuffs, and he was continually hitching up the cuffs as he paced up and down the piazza. He received his guests as they drove up to the horse block, and ushered them into the hotel.

We very seldom ate a meal at Wheeler's, but when we drove by on county fair days the delicious odors that came from the hotel kitchen and dining room made us look forward to eating our own lunch, which we carried in baskets.

One year, as we got to the gate of the fair grounds we heard the band playing "Marching through Georgia." The parading band boys were in red uniforms and red Turkish caps, led by a fat German bandmaster wielding his baton and at times turning sharply to face his band.

Bandsmen and barkers

Children of all descriptions were running along both sides of the band, some with little, round, "punkin" heads and putty noses with freckled bridges; some were carrying dolls, others marching in step with the band, sometimes stumbling along in their eagerness. A few were whimpering because they could not keep up and calling to their older brothers, "Wait for me!" I remember one falling flat on his stomach and losing hold of his balloon.

Soon the sound of the passing band was drowned by sideshow barkers shouting about the fat lady, the living skeleton, the snake charmer, the contortionist, the bearded lady, the sword- and fire-eater, the double-headed calf and the trained pigs!

In a semicircle reaching down to the racetrack were the shooting gallery, the tent where baseballs were thrown at the colored man's head and an outside stand where rings were tossed over canes, some of them having one- and five-dollar bills tied to them. Out in front of these sideshow tents and between them and the fair buildings, was the exhibition of agricultural equipment, consisting of mowing machines, plows, hay rakes, threshers, the latest type of hay presses, corn shellers, cider mills, reapers, pumps and windmills.

Worming their way through the crowds were boys and young men selling pink balls of popcorn smudged with sticky sweets and peanuts at five cents a bag.

Popcorn, sweets and peanuts

One peanut vendor, with a nasal voice, sang out, "Here's where you get your fresh roasted, humpbacked peanuts, raised on the farm of Henry Ward Beecher and picked by the forefinger of Jenny Lind and General Grant!" Another fellow was shouting, "Fresh lemonade, made in the shade, by an old maid and stirred with a stick."

We followed the procession of arriving wagons down to a field near the racetrack where countless rows of posts were set in the ground. Each had a heavy rail on top for tying the horses. Here we found one of the men authorized to tell where the horses should be unhitched, his authority being shown by the blue badge he wore. Gene Bradford, who was driving us, unhitched Fannie and Katie, removed their harness, put halters on and tied them to the rail. Then, with Mother and my two sisters we started on foot to use the hour before lunch for sightseeing.

Being least interested in the poultry house, we always visited that first. This was an isolated building, not very high. The poultry cages were open to the outside, so by going around the building the exhibits could be seen. There were also two rows inside, down the center.

In the cages were Shanghais, buff Cochins, Dominiques, Houdans, Plymouth Rocks, Bantams, white and brown Leghorns, turkeys and turkey gobblers, geese and ganders, ducks and drakes, guinea hens, peacocks, and usually one or two pens of guinea pigs.

As was to be expected, the farmers' wives took more interest in the poultry exhibit than did the men, since most birds had been raised by women. Their conversation covered the beauty as well as the defects of the poultry: diseases, and the cures for "leg weariness," "gapes" and other troubles. Young Mrs. Vridenburg was overheard to state to a friend, "The best way to cure the gapes is to take a loop of horsehair and run it down the chicken's throat and fish out the worm."

The interior of the building was full of dry dust from incessant scratching. The noise was awful from the crowing, squawking and cackling. The September air was stifling, yet the ladies were dressed in their best, from black silk to calico. Some protected their finery by wearing long linen dusters and tying silk handkerchiefs over their neck ruchings. Often, a small straw bonnet with a splatter of flowers or cherries was perched on a pile of puffs that sometimes failed to match the natural hair. Stiff corsets creaked as their wearers bent over to examine a hen or study the prize ribbons pinned on the cages.

From the poultry house we walked down through the exhibits of farm machinery and past the outside of the sideshows. Mother condescended to stop and look at the fat lady and the living skeleton only if they were on exhibit outside. We young ones longed to go in and see the inner mysteries but were limited to the trained pig exhibition.

The lunch hour finally arrived and we saw our cousins, all smiles, waving to us as we approached the carriages, where we soon sat side-by-side, feasting from our lunch baskets: roast chicken, thick ham and homemade bread sandwiches, potato salad, hardboiled eggs, pickles and jam, and cold coffee made rich with cream and sugar. For dessert there was mince or apple pie, chocolate and coconut layer cake, Alorris White peaches, Bartlett pears and Concord grapes as well as common ginger snaps.

Lunch and jolly laughter

We young ones ate all we could, growing jollier with every mouthful, and mother and Aunt Fannie could not help but laugh at our fun. Meanwhile, the horses ate their oats.

As we sat there eating, a homemade closed carriage drove up near us. The driver's seat was on the outside, the body of the carriage enclosed with common boards painted black over the sides and top. The windows were of small panes like little house windows, and the doors on each side were fitted with common house locks and white porcelain knobs. The bay horses were old and thin, as was the coachman who drove them.

The couple that emerged from the vehicle looked almost a hundred years old. The old lady was dressed in a flouncy, black dress and had three or four gray curls hanging from under her black bonnet and falling on each side of her face. She wore lace mitts on her hands. The old gentleman was in dark clothes, with a stovepipe hat on his iron-gray wig, which was several shades darker than his whiskers.

An aged couple

None of us knew who they were, where they came from or where they went.

After our luncheon visit we went to the agricultural hall, a large, plain building with entrance porches on three sides. On the fourth side the porch connected it with the floral hall. In agricultural hall were long rows of tables loaded with all kinds of fresh vegetables and fruits and other tables with glass jars of beautiful canned fruits and rows and rows of jars with delicious-looking preserves. The exhibitors, in white aprons, usually would be standing beside the jars, beaming with happiness and talking to friends.

Agricultural Hall

In other parts of the hall were sheaves of rye, barley and oats, and ears and stalks of field and sweet corn, many of which were used for decorating the beams and posts of the building. A little earlier in the season, during the harvest moon, the agricultural hall was the setting for the big annual agricultural picnic, dance and supper.

Now, the place was crowded with people slowly milling about and looking at the produce and at demonstrations of butter-making with the latest appliances, consisting of a fluted butter-worker and revolving barrel and swing churns, which superseded the paddle-and-bowl worker and dasher churn.

One corner of the hall was reserved for bee-keeping supplies and was of much interest to many people from the mountains. They liked to watch the bees working behind the glass-enclosed, modern hives and to study the specimens of strained honey, the dark from the buckwheat, the light from white clover and other blossoms.

Mingling with the crowd was Thompson Kelly, a tall man of about fifty, with gray chin whiskers and wearing a long linen duster and coarse cowhide shoes, with a broad-brimmed straw hat on his rather small head. On one arm he carried a small market basket covered with a red bandana handkerchief. If anyone showed the slightest curiosity about the basket's contents, Mr. Kelly would smilingly pull aside the handkerchief and show a large ostrich egg nestled in cotton batting.

Mr. Kelly's bandana

This same performance of Mr. Kelly's had been going on for years at the county fair.

Floral hall was an octagon, and along its outer edge were booths. The aisle between these booths and the center exhibition stands was a wide one, going around the entire building. One outside booth showed an exhibition of harnesses, another of side- bar, half-spring and full-spring buggies; other booths showed the very latest thing in rubber tires. In some booths were sales representatives with models of the farm machinery that stood outside.

Singer sewing machine models from the three-story Singer building at 16th Street and Union Square, New York City, filled a booth. Hardware and fishing tackle were in others, and in another were wooden and iron flower stands for garden use. The pastry and candy booth was a display from a manufacturer in Poughkeepsie. Among its wares were Smith Brothers cough drops (made locally, for the brothers lived here) and blue and green candy soldiers, four or five inches

high. Further on was a booth for Horton's ice cream, sold for ten cents a mound heaped on round china saucers. Then there was a booth with Columbia chilled plows, Lane plows and Syracuse plows.

On the inner side of the aisle was a rail to protect the high tables upon which were beautiful flower exhibits. One was reserved for roses and here we usually sent some of our own from the Jacquemont bed. Once, Mother devised a more elaborate flower exhibit called "Queen Victoria," which attracted much favorable attention. She had old Jesse Vridenburg make a little canopy with four columns and a hip roof. Goldenrod trimmed the columns, and roses and other plants banked the canopy. Set against a black velvet background was a beautiful wax doll, Queen Victoria in miniature, with purple and gold velvet robes, jewelled crown and gilded throne.

Further along in the floral hall was an exhibition of

potted plants such as white and yellow azaleas, night-blooming cereuses, variegated coleuses, white and yellow jasmines and pink and white primroses. Hanging back of the flower stands were gay patchwork quilts, beautifully made, as were many other samples of needlework that nearly surrounded the hall.

Garden lovers exhibited their beautiful calla lilies, verbenas, geraniums, asters, marigolds, portulacas, pansies, primroses and sunflowers. Wild flowers from the meadows, roadsides and woods were shown, such as the brown speckled, yellow meadow lilies, white bullseye daisies, boneset, goldenrod, large bunches of timothy and redtop grasses, creeping ground pine and white clematis from the stonewalls and fences.

Before one of these stands was a farm woman deeply interested in an exhibit of seeds and wanting a catalogue. The first I knew, she had, without looking, passed her sleeping child toward me, saying, "Here, James, take the baby!" To her surprise, James was several steps ahead in the crowd.

I get the baby

The goodnatured crowd was almost too thick for comfort, when from behind us we heard someone say to my sister, "How do you do, my dear?" She turned and saw old Chatterton, a harmless elderly tramp, well known throughout the county. He wore his customary costume over his short, thick-set figure—a conglomeration of patches from head to foot, yet clean and white, in effect. On his coat he had sewn hundreds of buttons, and he wore patched mittens the year 'round, but when shaking hands he always removed one and made a deep bow. Also part of his usual costume were green, gold-rimmed, corner-clipped spectacles. Beneath the spectacles his smooth-shaven face had a sweet, smiling expression.

Every once in a while, when darkness overtook him in our neighborhood, Chatterton would stop for a meal and a night's lodging in our barn. He was said to have lost his own farm years before, which had unsettled his reason and caused him to offer to buy every farm he visited. Milton Bostwick was the only one who ever accepted his offer. Then, old Chatterton was much taken aback and was silent for a time, finally saying he would go out and look it over.

He came back, shaking his head, and said he could not buy because the farm had the "tracks of a flat-footed goose" on it.

We children would have liked to have seen the morning horse races, with the two- and four-wheeled sulkies and the trotters with their bandaged legs and toe weights. Our time was too limited, however.

We were able, though, to see the, greatest novelty— the bicycle races, which began at two o'clock. About a dozen young men, dressed in knit jackets, knee breeches and bicycle stockings and shoes, mounted their high wheels with hard rubber tires, some with a little wheel behind, others with a little wheel in front. Some pedals made the full circle with the foot, others, with a compressor band, allowed the foot to go up and down only.

Bicycle races and balloon ascents

The big grandstand was full of excited spectators, the fences lined with them, cheering and clapping. To us, the riders' speed seemed something that could never be beaten on wheels on a racetrack.

In the distance I saw a gray object moving like an elephant, yet it was flabby and lopsided. Studying our program and examining the object more closely, we remembered that Mademoiselle Carlotta was almost due to make an ascent, and this was her hot-air balloon.

I was eager to see it, so my mother laughed and said we might go where we pleased but she was tired and must go back and rest in the carriage. My sisters went off toward the bandstand, where there were lectures, and I hurried as fast as I could toward the balloon.

By the time I got there, it was nearly inflated, but there was still a long wait. Finally, Mademoiselle Carlotta came out of the crowd, carrying a fur-trimmed, short coat and a pair of overshoes, which she calmly tossed into the basket of the balloon. The large, red-faced manager of the affair walked around the edge of the crowd surrounding the balloon and picked out strong and solid boys and men to hold the trailing lines. To my joy, I was one of the chosen ones, as I was large for my age.

We all hung on while Mademoiselle Carlotta pulled a gay toboggan cap down over her hair and lifted her traveling dress to climb into the basket of the balloon. The row of ballast bags was unhooked from the basket, and then the whole strain of holding down the balloon was upon us, a small task for so many.

We had been coached to listen for the signal, "Let go!" and with it the balloon started swaying gently upward over the crowd, Mademoiselle Carlotta looking down upon the upturned faces and waving her white handkerchief. To us she seemed a dream of beauty.

A dream of beauty

In less than an hour, Mademoiselle Carlotta and her balloon had landed near Pondgut, a long streak of water between two ponds, and she was out of my life forever.

The cattle stables, sheep and hog pens were the only places left to visit, and there was need to hurry because it was getting late in the afternoon. By now, there were not so many sightseers around the cattle pens. Several groups of farmers, awkwardly smoking their holiday cigars, were talking over the points of the different animals. Jim Robinson, a raiser of Shorthorns, was scratching his prize cow under her chin and asking one of the judges, "Hain't she a pretty head on her?"

On exhibit were Durhams, Holsteins, Jerseys, Guernseys and shorthorn cattle. Some of the cows were mooing while their calves were frisking about the pens. Bulls were answering each other in low, angry bellows. The more ferocious ones were tied by two ropes run through the rings in their noses. When the bulls were taken out of the pen for any purpose, they would be led from one side by a man with a long hickory staff snapped in the nose ring, and from the other side by a man leading with a rope. The bulls were easy to lead this way because the copper rings made their noses tender.

Cattle and sheep

The sheep pens were mostly filled with Merinos and Southdowns. Some ugly rams, with crooked horns and expressionless eyes, bunted against the boards of their pens. Very few people seemed interested to visit the sheep pens. More of a crowd surrounded the sheds where the hog pens were. Black Berkshires, white Chesters and Poland China hogs lay snoring, and this caused the visitors to talk softly as they tiptoed through.

The close of a perfect day

At the end of the day, the shadows were getting long as the procession of wagons and carriages began to leave the fairgrounds. The remaining horses were beginning to get uneasy, some pawing and digging holes under their feet, others whinnying, thinking they spied their mates in the distance. Even old horses that had rested all day were champing at their bits.

As our wagon approached the exit gate, there stood colored Mary Watson, big and fat, waiting for her turn to go through. Her broad-brimmed straw hat was trimmed with a wreath of artificial grass, and since she was standing very near Fannie's head, Fannie reached out to take a bite of the grass, sniffing in Mary's ear at the same time.

With a most unearthly yell, Mary ducked to one side, shivering and shaking. As she walked out of the gate, she frequently rolled her eyes back at the horse, until she was lost in the crowd.

Later, we stopped to water the horses at Husted's drinking trough, and as the sky was overcast it was almost too dark to see the road. Driving on, over the crown of O'Brien's hill, we could see a light streak of sky as the moon came out. From where I sat in the back seat, Gene's head was outlined against the moon as he drove.

Gene speaks for all of us

Mother said, "Eugene, have you enjoyed the day?"

Gene spoke for all of us, answering with a satisfied, "Yes'm!"

A silhouette of Benson Lossing was cut in 1876.

ABOUT BENSON J. LOSSING, HISTORIAN

Thomas Lossing's devoted father, Benson John Lossing, squire of The Ridge in Dutchess County, New York, was a true 19th Century *portmanteau* man—illustrator, writer, editor, historian—and is said to have done more than any other person to popularize the subject of the history of the United States.

Benson was descended from Pietre Pieterse Lassingh, a Dutch brewer who settled in Albany, New York in 1658. He sold his business in 1681 and moved to the Dutchess County shore of the Hudson River. Benson was born in the town of Beekman on February 12, 1813 to John and Miriam (Dorland) Lossing. His father died the year Benson was born and his mother died when he was not quite 12, thus ending his formal schooling after only three years. He was then apprenticed to a Poughkeepsie watchmaker. Though his teen years were harsh ones, he found time to read and study, especially in the field of history, which fascinated him.

When he was 22, Benson became a partner in and joint editor of *The Poughkeepsie Telegraph,* one of the largest country weekly newspapers in the state, with a circulation of 2,300. Thus began a writing career that was to span nearly 60 years. The next year, 1836, *The Telegraph* owners began publishing the *Poughkeepsie Casket,* a fortnightly literary journal, of which Benson was also co-editor. This was a time when women's magazines and inexpensive literary weeklies, usually called "caskets" or "repositories" were springing up all over the country. They usually featured stories, poetry, ladies' departments and many articles under the headings of "Variety" or "Miscellany," as well as marriage and death notices under the captions "The Knot" and "The Knell." The *Poughkeepsie Casket* was of that order, but also contained many historical and biographical sketches written by Benson Lossing. These were illustrated with wood engravings made by him. This was a craft he had learned from J.A. Adams, who drew illustrations for the *Casket.*

In 1838, Benson moved to New York City where he established himself as a wood engraver, in addition to continuing to edit the Poughkeepsie newspapers. From 1839-41 he also edited the weekly *Family Magazine,* one of the nation's first pictorial magazines. Ever prolific as a writer, he found time also to write his first book, *Outline History of the Fine Arts,* which was published in 1840 as part of Harper's Family Library.

His popularity grew and he produced many engravings and articles for various periodicals. For local journals in particular he wrote biographical and historical articles, preserving the recollections of the older people around him of life in Colonial and Revolutionary times. His published illustrations are today the only ones extant of many old buildings now demolished.

Benson Lossing engravings appeared also in most of the job-printing work done by the Poughkeepsie Telegraph Press, such as programs, school catalogs and circulars of all kinds. For many years he and William Barritt conducted the largest wood engraving business in New York and supplied some of the best examples of that art to the books and periodicals of the day.

In his writings, Benson frequently advocated the establishment of "neighborhood libraries." His idea was that residents of community would pool their collections of books for reading during, the winter months, "by which scheme a large library might be formed for mutual benefit."

He was long-interested in the education of women and wrote many articles about the subject. He was a friend of Matthew Vassar and was a trustee of Vassar College from its establishment in 1861 until his death in 1891. In 1867, he wrote and illustrated the monograph, "Vassar College and Its Founder."

On June 26, 1833, Benson married Alice Barritt, who shared his literary interests and wrote for New York newspapers. She died April 18, 1855. On November 8, 1856, Benson married Helen Sweet, daughter of Nehemiah Sweet. They had four children, Edwin, Miriam Helen, Thomas and Alice.

In 1868, Benson Lossing purchased a 300-hundred-acre farm atop Chestnut Ridge, above the town of Dover Plains. He called his home The Ridge. Next to the house he built a fireproof granite, two-story library for his collection of 5,000 books. Along with them was his collection of historical treasures, said to include a portion of Martha Washington's wedding dress, a piece of curtain brought over on the Mayflower, a piece of the flag flown at Fort Sumter and a cane made from the wood of Perry's flagship in the battle of Lake Erie.

Lossing was a prolific writer virtually all his adult life. In 1848 he conceived the idea of writing a narrative sketchbook about the scenes and sights of the American Revolution. He obtained an author's advance from Harper & Brothers. Altogether, he covered 8,000 miles in the United States and Canada over a period of five years, gathering material and sketching. His *Pictorial Field Book of the American Revolution*, still used by scholars for its wealth of details, was published in parts between 1850-52.

Over the years, he turned out more than 40 titles of history and biography, among them, *Our Countrymen, or Brief Memoirs of Eminent Americans* (1855), *The Hudson, from the Wilderness to the Sea* (1866), *The Life and Times of Philip Schuyler* (1860-73), *Pictorial Fieldbook of the War of 1812* (1868), *Pictorial History of the Civil War* (1866-68), *Our Country* (1876-78), *A Biography of James A. Garfield* (1882), *History of New York City* (1884) and *The Empire State* (1887).

He spent the rest of his life at The Ridge. He was described in later life as being of medium height, stockily built, with kindly features and a ruddy complexion. Of him, it was said he accomplished his writing "without the spasmodic outbursts characteristic of writers of the nervous type." He continued working until the time of his death, June 3, 1891, in his 79th year.

Benson Lossing's funeral was held at Christ Church, Poughkeepsie and he was buried in the Poughkeepsie Rural Cemetery.

ACKNOWLEDGEMENTS

My thanks go to Great Uncle Thomas and Aunt Bess Lossing for leaving to posterity this fascinating memoir.

Stuart Murray, as associate editor, provided invaluable guidance in the development of this project and brought his keen eye for detail to our research about the Lossing family.

Thanks, too, go to Wray Rominger of Purple Mountain Press for publishing Thomas Lossing's memoir.

John H. Rhodehamel, curator of American history at the Huntington Library, San Marino, California, and Virginia J. Renner, reader services librarian, and their staff were most helpful in the course of my research, and the Huntington Library kindly gave its permission to reprint several Benson Lossing sketches in this volume.

Nan Card of the Rutherford B. Hayes Presidential Center, Spiegel Grove, Ohio, generously provided copies of Lossing family correspondence.

The Dutchess County Historical Society, Poughkeepsie, New York, gave its permission to use excerpts from the memoir published in its 1946 and 1947 Yearbooks.

P.D.H.